WEDDING CAKES

by Rosalind Miller

CONTENTS

Introduction

One day in 2005, after returning from a trip to New York and tasting one of the famous Magnolia Bakery's cupcakes, I left my job as a lecturer in graphic design at Central Saint Martins School of Art and Design, and started making cakes. People around me thought I was mad (and for a moment I suspected they were right), but in fact the cake baking and decorating bug had been with me my entire life.

My mother was a dedicated cake decorating hobbyist; making beautiful traditional sugar flowers to adorn birthday cakes, un-birthday cakes, and any possible event that could be celebrated with cake! I vividly remember my mother and my aunt trying to out-do each other with their delicious macaroons, chocolate eclairs, strudels and decorated savoury pies; each one more elaborate than the last. Of course, there was an enormous amount of fun to be had by us kids as we all mucked in and attempted our own little creations.

As I grew older, I transferred my creativity to studying art, first with a BA and a Masters in textiles and later an MA in communication design at Central St Martins. Even then cakes were in the back of my mind. I remember spending hours making a wooden and Perspex cake structure filled with dried fruit and decorated with piped plaster of Paris. I went on to try my hand at different artistic endeavours including teaching art, setting up an art gallery, being a fine artist, founding a digital design company, and then lecturing at Central Saint Martins. I was very creative but also very restless, constantly searching for new challenges. Then, one day I found my mother's old notebooks from the classes she used to take in sugar-craft and cake-decorating. This started my brain ticking over; it was a creative pursuit that came from a deep family tradition, which I had not yet experimented with. A few years later I found myself walking away from my job and embarking on a career in cake-making, and suddenly everything seemed to click into place.

My first ventures into cake-making as a career were with my sister, Julie. The trend for cupcakes had not yet exploded, and whilst the ones from Magnolia were delicious, they were very simply decorated. We wondered how far you could go with decorations on a cupcake, and began experimenting. After trying out different recipes, we baked 100 cakes and with the help of my two sisters, daughter and niece, set upon the task of making the most extravagantly decorated cupcakes that we could imagine. We took up a pitch at Greenwich Market to sell them, and were soon inundated with customers.

This newly embraced love of cake-decorating naturally progressed into making wedding cakes, and brought me to where I am today.

With Rosalind Miller Cakes, my aim was always to make cakes that were each their own individual work of art. I didn't want to replicate traditional cake decorating styles or base my ideas on existing designs; I wanted to carve my own unique path, approaching cake design as I would any other art project.

When people come to me for their wedding cake, they are usually looking for an original statement piece that reflects their own individuality. Of course, traditionally popular wedding cake styles and decorations, such as sugar flowers, will always endure no matter what the fashion for wedding cakes is; but the key to making a stunning and unique wedding cake is how you approach the overall design, rather than the separate elements.

My advice for anyone embarking on a project like this is to always keep a sketchbook to hand. Whilst the process sometimes feels random, a new cake design often evolves over a number of weeks, growing and developing from moments of inspiration; a lace pattern on a dress, a visit to a historic house or flowers in the garden. Snap photos, sketch ideas, look out for colours that work together; anything can inspire you.

You sometimes can't tell if something will work. Or at least not until you have tried it. Therefore I play around with the design as much as possible beforehand; stacking dummy tiers to work out the right shape of the cake, mocking up and cutting out design ideas on paper, and experimenting with colour schemes to see what works and what doesn't.

I always offer my clients a consultation, during which they can taste different flavours of cake, discuss ideas, and cover everything we need to design the perfect cake that works best for their wedding. These are some questions I ask my clients during the consultation:

- How many guests does the cake need to serve, and therefore, how big will it need to be?
- Is there a dessert being served, or will the cake be the dessert? This will determine the portion size. I offer a 2.5cm x 2.5cm x 10cm portion size to serve with coffee, or a 2.5cm x 5cm x 10cm portion size as a dessert.
- What is the venue like? A small cake will look lost in a grand ballroom with high ceilings. The cake can be made taller by using some dummy tiers.
- Is there a particular theme or colour scheme being used for the wedding?
- What is the client's personal style?

It's also important to consider how the cake will be transported and set up at the venue. Depending on the design and the timing of the wedding, you may opt to take it as separate tiers and assemble it there, or stack the cake first and drive extremely slowly! I usually transport my cakes in a cardboard box, which is the same size as the base-board, so the cake can't move around inside the box. The box is then placed on a piece of non-slip matting in the back of the van. The finished cakes can be very heavy, so make sure you have some help.

My aim was to write a book that would not only serve as a cake decorating technical manual, but also as an inspirational springboard for your own ideas. I've included all the basics; tried and tested cake recipes; instructions on how to fill, trim and cover a cake for a professional finish; and a guide to

assembling a tiered wedding cake, alongside step-by-step imagery. You'll find useful hints and tips that I have learned and developed over the years to aide the process.

The main part of the book is made up of detailed breakdowns of 11 wedding cake designs. I chose these projects because they have been some of my favourites, and also because they display a wide variety of techniques and styles. The flower techniques are separate to the cakes, and the various other techniques (piping, painting etc), are also clearly indicated in each project. I hope that this way you will feel comfortable to either make the cakes as I have made them, or to take bits from each one and mix and match to suit your own vision and create your own wedding cake design.

Making a wedding cake takes time and patience and a lot of hard work. But when all the elements come together in a way that really expresses who you are and what your wedding is all about, it can be a uniquely rewarding enterprise. I wish you many happy adventures in wedding cakes!

Rosalind Miller

RECIPES

Baking tips and techniques

Although a wedding cake has to look spectacular on the outside, it's just as important that it tastes good too. Bear these tips for baking in mind, and you won't go wrong.

BASICS

- Always use the best quality and freshest ingredients you can find. I try to use organic and fair trade wherever possible.

- I prefer to use natural flavourings; the freshly grated zest of a lemon, good quality vanilla bean paste, extract, or seeds scraped from fresh vanilla pods, or fresh raspberries. If you can only get flavourings, then look for natural extracts rather than "essences" which are often made with artificial ingredients.

- It's always best to use a flour specifically marketed as "cake" or "sponge" flour. This flour has a lower gluten content than regular flour, and will produce a lighter, softer cake.

- Eggs should be weighed without their shell.

- I always use unsalted butter, as this is fresher than salted. You can substitute some of the butter for a baking margarine if you prefer.

- Most cakes will last at least one week from baking, and can be baked in advance, wrapped in clingfilm and frozen. For a Saturday wedding cake, I would usually bake the cake on Tuesday; torte, fill, trim and crumbcoat and marzipan or ganache on Wednesday; sugarpaste on Thursday and decorate on Friday.

BAKING TECHNIQUES

- Always use your ingredients at room temperature, not straight from the fridge.

- Ensure your butter is soft, but not melted.

- Unless the recipe states otherwise, cream together the butter and sugar (beating in a mixer or by hand) until the mixture is light and fluffy.

- Always sift your flour. This gets rid of lumps and helps incorporate air.

- Always fold in the flour and milk very, very gently, just mixing with a metal spoon until the flour or milk is incorporated. Your folding technique is very important – use a large metal spoon to scrape the base of the bowl, then twist it in a folding motion as it is lifted and then put it back into the mix. The most common reason for cakes failing is over-beating at this stage.

- Grease and line your tins with baking or greaseproof paper.

- For large cakes, 25cm and over, it is advisable to fold some brown paper to the height of the tin, and wrap it around the outside of the tin. This will help prevent the edges burning before the inside is thoroughly cooked.

- Always test your cakes at the end of the cooking time by inserting a clean knife. They are cooked when the knife comes out clean.

- And don't forget to heat the oven up first!

Cakes

Each tier of a wedding cake is comprised of four layers. The cakes are baked in two tins, then sliced in half horizontally, creating four layers.

VANILLA SPONGE

Ingredients

To make a 20cm round cake

- 2 x 20cm x 7.5cm high round tins
- 480g unsalted butter
- 540g caster sugar
- 480g eggs (approx 8 large eggs)
- 480g self-raising cake flour
- 1 tsp vanilla extract
- 60ml milk

Method

1. Heat up your oven to 130°C on a fan-assisted oven, or 150° on a regular oven (gas mark 2).
2. Cream together the softened butter and caster sugar until it's light and fluffy (this takes about five minutes in a stand mixer).
3. Sift the flour into a separate bowl.
4. Add the eggs one at a time, beating well between each one. If the mix starts to curdle, add a teaspoon of flour with each egg.
5. Add the vanilla extract and beat for 20 seconds more.
6. Fold in ⅓ of the flour.
7. Fold in ½ of the milk.
8. Fold in ⅓ of the flour.
9. Fold in ½ of the milk.
10. Fold in the last ⅓ of the flour.
11. Pour the mixture into the two lined 20cm cake tins and bake until cooked (approx 1hr 20min).

LEMON SPONGE

Ingredients

To make a 20cm round cake

- 2 x 20cm x 7.5cm high round tins
- 480g unsalted butter
- 540g caster sugar
- 480g eggs (approx 8 large eggs)
- 480g self-raising cake flour
- Zest of 4 lemons
- 60ml milk

Method

1. Heat up your oven to 130°C on a fan-assisted oven, or 150° on a regular oven (gas mark 2).
2. Cream together the softened butter and caster sugar until it's light and fluffy (this takes about five minutes in a stand mixer).
3. Sift the flour into a separate bowl.
4. Add the eggs one at a time, beating well between each one. If the mix starts to curdle, add a teaspoon of flour with each egg.
5. Add lemon zest and beat for 20 seconds more.
6. Fold in ⅓ of the flour.
7. Fold in ½ of the milk.
8. Fold in ⅓ of the flour.
9. Fold in ½ of the milk.
10. Fold in the last ⅓ of the flour.
11. Pour the mixture into the two lined 20cm cake tins and bake until cooked (approx 1hr 20min).

CHOCOLATE SPONGE

Ingredients

To make a 20cm round cake

- 2 x 20cm x 7.5cm high round tins
- 480g unsalted butter
- 540g caster sugar
- 480g eggs (approx 8 large eggs)
- 360g self-raising cake flour
- 1 tsp vanilla extract
- 120g good quality cocoa powder
- 60ml milk

Method

1. Heat up your oven to 130°C on a fan-assisted oven, or 150° on a regular oven (gas mark 2).
2. Cream together the softened butter and caster sugar until it's light and fluffy (this takes about five

minutes in a stand mixer).

3. Sift the flour and cocoa into a separate bowl.
4. Add the eggs one at a time, beating well between each one. If the mix starts to curdle, add a teaspoon of flour with each egg.
5. Add the vanilla extract and beat for 20 seconds more.
6. Fold in ⅓ of the flour and cocoa.
7. Fold in ½ of the milk.
8. Fold in ⅓ of the flour and cocoa.
9. Fold in ½ of the milk.
10. Fold in the last ⅓ of the flour and cocoa.
12. Pour the mixture into the two lined 20cm cake tins and bake until cooked (approx 1hr 20min).

RASPBERRY AND VANILLA SPONGE

Ingredients
To make a 20cm round cake
- 2 x 20cm x 7.5cm high round tins
- 480g unsalted butter
- 540g caster sugar
- 480g eggs (approx 8 large eggs)
- 480g self-raising cake flour
- 1 tsp vanilla extract
- 60ml milk
- 200g fresh raspberries

Method
1. Heat up your oven to 130°C on a fan-assisted oven, or 150° on a regular oven (gas mark 2).
2. Cream together the softened butter and caster sugar until it's light and fluffy (this takes about five minutes in a stand mixer).
3. Sift the flour into a separate bowl.
4. Add the eggs one at a time, beating well between each one. If the mix starts to curdle, add a teaspoon of flour with each egg.
5. Add the vanilla extract and beat for 20 seconds more.
6. Fold in ⅓ of the flour.
7. Fold in ½ of the milk.
8. Fold in ⅓ of the flour.
9. Fold in ½ of the milk.
10. Fold in the last ⅓ of the flour.
11. Fold in the raspberries.
12. Pour the mixture into the two lined 20cm cake tins and bake until cooked (approx 1hr 20min).

RED VELVET

This is a popular American cake that has a red sponge. Usually made as cupcakes, it works just as well for a larger cake.

Ingredients
To make a 20cm round cake
- 2 x 20cm x 7.5cm high round tins
- 200g unsalted butter
- 460g caster sugar
- 240g eggs (approx 4 large eggs)
- 500g plain cake flour
- 2 tsp vanilla extract
- 400ml buttermilk
- 20ml liquid red food colouring
- 1½ tsp bicarbonate of soda
- 1½ tsp baking powder
- 1½ tsp white wine vinegar
- 1 tsp salt
- 25g cocoa powder

Method
1. Heat up your oven to 130°C on a fan-assisted oven, or 150° on a regular oven (gas mark 2).
2. Add the red food colour and vinegar to lukewarm buttermilk in a jug and stir until mixed.
3. Sift your dry ingredients (flour, bicarbonate of soda, baking powder, salt and cocoa) together in a large bowl.
4. Cream together the softened butter and caster sugar until light and fluffy (about five minutes in a stand mixer).
5. Add the eggs one at a time, beating well between each one. If the mix starts to curdle, add a teaspoon of flour with each egg.
6. Add the vanilla extract, and beat for 20 seconds more.
7. Fold in ⅓ of the dry ingredients mixture.
8. Fold in ½ of the buttermilk mixture.
9. Fold in ⅓ of the dry ingredients mixture.
10. Fold in ½ the buttermilk mixture.
11. Fold in the last ⅓ of the dry ingredients.
12. Pour the mixture into the two lined 20cm cake tins and bake until cooked (approx 1hr 20min).

RICH FRUITCAKE

This is the traditional recipe for wedding cakes. If wrapped well in greaseproof paper and tinfoil, the cake can be kept for up to a year, and it's customary to keep the top tier for the christening of the first child or the first wedding anniversary.

Make your fruitcakes at least six weeks in advance so that they have time to mature. A mature fruitcake cuts well and doesn't crumble.

Ingredients
To make a 20cm round cake
- 1 x 20cm x 7.5cm high round tin
- 575g currants
- 225g sultanas
- 225g raisins
- 60g glacé cherries
- 60g mixed peel
- 60ml brandy (or cognac, armagnac, rum or sherry)
- 275g plain flour
- ½ tsp salt
- ½ tsp freshly grated nutmeg
- ¾ tsp mixed spice
- 60g chopped almonds or other nuts to taste
- 275g soft brown sugar
- 1 tbsp black treacle
- 275g unsalted butter
- 300g egg (about 5 large eggs)
- Zest of 1 lemon
- Zest of 1 large orange

Method
1. Two days before baking, put the fruit and peel in a large bowl and cover with the brandy (or other alcohol). Leave to soak for 48 hours.
2. Heat up your oven to 120°C on a fan-assisted oven, or 140° on a regular oven (gas mark 1).
3. Sift the dry ingredients (flour, salt and spices) together in a large bowl.
4. Cream together the softened butter and sugar until light and fluffy (about five minutes in a stand mixer).
5. Add the eggs one at a time, beating well between each one. If the mix starts to curdle, add a teaspoon of flour with each egg.
6. Fold in the dry ingredients (flour, salt and spices).
7. Add the soaked fruit and peel, nuts, treacle and lemon and orange zest. Heat a spoon before measuring out the treacle - this will make it slide easily off the spoon.
8. Pour the mixture into a lined cake tin. Wrap the outside of the tin with brown paper and tie. Cover the top of the cake with a double layer of greaseproof paper with a small hole cut out of the middle.
9. Bake until cooked (approx 4hrs for a 20cm cake, 3hrs for a 15cm cake, 5 hrs for a 23cm cake, or 5½hrs for a 25.5cm cake).

For other size cakes multiply the ingredients for a 20cm cake by the following amounts:

For 12.5cm (5") round multiply by 0.4
For 15cm (6") round multiply by 0.6
For 18cm (7") round multiply by 0.8
For 23cm (9") round multiply by 1.3
For 25.5cm (10") round multiply by 1.6
For 28cm (11") round multiply by 2
For 30cm (12") round multiply by 2.25
For 33cm (13") round multiply by 2.6
For 35.5cm (14") round multiply by 3.1

For 12.5cm (5") square multiply by 0.5
For 15cm (6") square multiply by 0.7
For 18cm (7") square multiply by 1
For 20cm (8") square multiply by 1.3
For 23cm (9") square multiply by 1.6
For 25.5cm (10") square multiply by 2
For 28cm (11") square multiply by 2.4
For 30cm (12") square multiply by 3
For 33cm (13") square multiply by 3.4
For 35.5cm (14") square multiply by 4

For 12.5cm (5") hexagon multiply by 0.2
For 15cm (6") hexagon multiply by 0.35
For 18cm (7") hexagon multiply by 0.6
For 20cm (8") hexagon multiply by 0.8
For 23cm (9") hexagon multiply by 1
For 25.5cm (10") hexagon multiply by 1.3
For 28cm (11") hexagon multiply by 1.6
For 30cm (12") hexagon multiply by 2
For 33cm (13") hexagon multiply by 2.2
For 35.5cm (14") hexagon multiply by 2.5

Fillings and syrups

Applying syrups and fillings between each layer will keep your cake moist and flavourful.

VANILLA BUTTERCREAM

Ingredients
- 250g unsalted butter
- 400g icing sugar
- 50ml of milk
- 1 h vanilla extract

Method
1. Beat the butter for about five minutes in a stand mixer until it becomes much paler and fluffy.
2. Add the icing sugar one spoonful at a time and beat on a low speed until incorporated with the butter. Drape a towel over the mixer so the icing sugar doesn't fly all over your kitchen.
3. Add the milk and vanilla extract, and beat for another five minutes.

CHOCOLATE BUTTERCREAM

Ingredients
- 250g unsalted butter
- 300g icing sugar
- 100g cocoa powder
- 50ml of milk
- 1 tsp vanilla extract

Method
1. Beat the butter for about five minutes in a stand mixer until it becomes much paler in colour and fluffy.
2. Add the icing sugar one spoonful at a time and beat on a low speed until incorporated with the butter.
3. Add the cocoa powder and beat on a low speed until incorporated with the butter.
4. Add the milk and beat for another five minutes.

LEMON BUTTERCREAM

Ingredients
- 250g unsalted butter
- 400g icing sugar
- 90ml of lemon juice

Method
1. Beat the butter for about five minutes in a stand mixer until it becomes much paler and fluffy.
2. Add the icing sugar one spoonful at a time and beat on a low speed until incorporated with the butter. Drape a towel over the mixer so the icing sugar doesn't fly all over your kitchen.
3. Add the lemon juice and beat for another five minutes.

LEMON CURD

Ingredients
- Zest and juice of 4 lemons
- 125g unsalted butter
- 450g caster sugar
- 12 eggs
- 800 ml milk

Method
1. Put all ingredients in saucepan.
2. Whisk continuously over a low heat until thick.

WEDDING CAKES

CHOCOLATE GANACHE

Chocolate ganache is usually used as an undercoat for sponge cakes, but you can also add it to chocolate buttercream for an extra rich flavour.

Ingredients
- 250ml whipping cream
- 500g plain couverture chocolate (minimum 55% cocoa)

Method
1. Break the chocolate into small pieces
2. Heat the cream in a saucepan until it just reaches boiling point.
3. Pour over the chocolate pieces and using a hand whisk, whisk until the chocolate is melted. Then leave to cool.

LEMON SUGAR SYRUP

Ingredients
- 2 tbsp of caster sugar
- 60ml of fresh lemon juice

Method
1. Gently heat the caster sugar and lemon juice in a saucepan until all the sugar has dissolved.

VANILLA SUGAR SYRUP

Ingredients
- 2 tbsp of caster sugar
- 50ml of water
- 2 tsp vanilla extract

Method
1. Gently heat the caster sugar, water and vanilla extract in a saucepan until all the sugar has dissolved.

TIP
You can also experiment with other syrup flavours. Try adding coffee, lime juice or rosewater to the sugar as alternatives.

Covering and decorating

SUGARPASTE

Also known as fondant, sugarpaste is your basic cake covering material. I usually buy this readymade, but here are some recipes if you want to make your own.

Ingredients
- 900g icing sugar
- ¼ cup water
- 1 tbsp gelatin
- ½ cup glucose
- 1½ tbsp glycerin
- Any flavouring or colour to taste

Method
1. Put the gelatin in the water in a double boiling pan and heat very gently, just until it dissolves.
2. Sieve the icing sugar into a large bowl and make a well in the centre.
3. Add the glucose and glycerine to the dissolved gelatin and mix well.
4. Pour this mixture into the well and mix, first with a spoon and then your hands until you have a nice consistency.
5. Add flavouring and colour and mix again.
6. You can keep this sugarpaste in the refrigerator in an airtight container for three months.

MARSHMALLOW SUGARPASTE

Marshmallow sugarpaste has a lovely smell and a marshmallow-y taste that some people prefer. It does tend to get stickier and moister than regular sugarpaste so can be a little harder to work with.

Ingredients
- 450g white mini marshmallows
- 130g white vegetable fat
- 900g icing sugar
- 2½ tbsp warm water
- Food colouring as desired

What to do
1. Melt the marshmallows with 2½ tablespoons of water in a double boiler.
2. If you want to colour your sugarpaste, add it in now.
3. Place ¾ of the icing sugar on the top of the melted marshmallow mix.
4. Grease the mixer bowl with white vegetable fat, and mix with the rest of the icing sugar until a ball forms.
5. Cover with white vegetable fat, then wrap in clingfilm and store in the fridge. It will keep for three months.

MODELLING PASTE

Modelling paste is made from sugarpaste and an edible gum (Tylo powder). This strengthens the paste and makes it more pliable and stretchy, making it easier to shape for more substantial decorations.

Ingredients
- 250g sugarpaste
- 1 tsp Tylo powder (a.k.a. CMC or Carboxymethylcellulose)

Method
1. Knead the Tylo powder well into the sugarpaste.
2. Wrap well in clingfilm or a plastic bag and leave to rest for one hour before using. You can add more Tylo powder if you want a stiffer paste.

FLOWER PASTE

This is the basic modeling material for all your flowers and decorations. It can be rolled out to a translucent thinness and dries hard. I usually buy my flower paste readymade, but this is a good recipe if you want to make your own.

Ingredients
- 450g sieved icing sugar,
- 1 tsp gum tragacanth
- 4 tsp Tylo powder (a.k.a. CMC or Carboxymethylcellulose)
- 2 tsp white vegetable fat
- 2 tsp powdered gelatine
- 5 tsp (25ml) cold water
- 2 tsp liquid glucose
- 9 tsp (45ml) egg white

Method
1. Grease a bowl with white vegetable fat, and sieve the icing sugar into it.
2. Add the Tylo powder and gum tragacanth to the sieved icing sugar.
3. Warm this mixture in a microwave for three bursts of 20 seconds, or until the sugar feels just warm.
4. Pour 25ml of water into a small bowl and sprinkle the gelatin on top of it. Leave it for ten minutes. It should take on a spongy appearance.
5. Place this bowl in hot water, until it goes clear.
6. Add the white vegetable fat and the glucose.
7. Take this mixture and pour it into the warmed sugar. Add the egg white to this and beat.
8. Keep beating until the mixture becomes white and stringy. This can be done in the mixer using a dough hook.
9. Turn onto a work surface. Grease your hands with white vegetable fat and knead it all together.
10. Wrap in clingfilm and then a freezer bag and let it rest for 24 hours before using.
11. When you're ready to use the flower paste, knead it out a bit. If it dries out, rub a little white vegetable fat into your hands before you knead.

EDIBLE GLUE

Ingredients
- ¼ tsp Tylo powder (a.k.a. CMC or Carboxymethyl cellulose)
- 15ml boiled water

Method
1. Mix the Tylo powder and boiled water in a small jar with a lid. Shake well to mix, and leave for one hour until the powder is dissolved.

ROYAL ICING

Royal icing is a smooth, white icing that dries very hard. It is used for attaching decorations, piped decorations and on top of dowels when stacking tiers.

Ingredients
- 1 egg white
- 250g icing sugar
- 1 tsp lemon juice

Method
1. Beat all ingredients together on the slow speed of a stand mixer for around five minutes.
2. Add lemon juice drop by drop to get a looser consistency if needed.
3. Cover the bowl with a clean damp cloth to prevent air getting to the icing and crusting it over.

HOW TO MAKE A PIPING BAG

1. Take a 25cm square of baking paper and fold it diagonally in half. Cut along the fold so you have two triangles.
2. Take the two corners at either end of the long edge, and fold them into each other so they overlap, creating a point at the centre of the long edge.
3. Holding the point in place, keep sliding the two ends, until they overlap with the bit that is sticking up.
4. Fold over the three sticking-up layers in towards the centre.
5. Then make a small tear either side of the overlap and fold this part in towards the centre. This will keep the bag from coming apart.
6. Snip off 1cm from the point of the cone and insert your piping nozzle.
7. Fill your piping bag so it's about ⅓ full, and then gently push the icing down to the bottom. Fold the sides in to the centre and then fold the top down.

TIPS

- Always pipe some tests to check you have consistency of the icing correct for the piping tip you are using. As a general rule, the smaller the tip, the looser the icing should be.
- Thin the icing to the correct consistency by adding lemon juice, a drop at a time.
- I usually make my royal icing quite loose when piping dots and pearls, as you can then achieve a lovely smooth pearl without annoying peaks.
- It's best to make royal icing on the day it will be used.

GENERAL
TECHNIQUES

Torting, filling and covering a cake

Equipment needed

- / Large non-stick rolling pin
- / Sugarpaste (see chart on p. 36 for amounts needed)
- / Marzipan (see chart on p. 36 for amounts needed)
- / Buttercream (see p. 16 for recipe)
- / Chocolate ganache (see p. 19 for recipe)
- / Icing sugar
- / Marzipan spacers
- / Large knife
- / Small paring knife
- / Tape measure
- / Set square
- / Offset spatula
- / Silicone pastry brush
- / Cake turntable
- / Cake smoothers
- / Cake boards and drums
- / Plastic dowels
- / Garden pruners (kept just for cakes to cut dowels)
- / Spirit level

To start

1. Bake your cakes and leave them to cool. You can wrap them in a double layer of clingfilm and freeze them. This has the advantage of allowing you to bake in advance, and also helps make the cakes a bit moister and firmer – making them easier to handle. If you do go this route, it's good to level and trim the cakes before they have completely defrosted – ie. still slightly frozen or at least very cold.

TORTING AND FILLING

Torting a cake means slicing it into horizontal layers so that you can add a filling, which will help the flavour as well ask keeping the cake moist.

1. Bake two 5cm high cakes for each tier. This will give you a deep 10cm high cake with four layers.

2. Use a cake leveller to cut each cake into two 2.5cm high layers. Remove the top and discard.

3. Take the cake board, which should be the same size as your cake tin, and spread a small amount of buttercream on it. Invert (flip over) the top layer of the cake and place it on the board (so the top of the cake is now at the bottom).

4. Make a sugar syrup (see recipes on p. 19) and gently spread this over the layer with a silicone pastry brush.

5. Use a palette knife to spread a thin layer of your chosen filling on top of the syrup, then invert the next layer on top of it.

6. Torte the second cake as before and continue until you have four layers of cake and three fillings, which can vary to taste. If I am making a vanilla cake, I make the first filling vanilla buttercream, the second raspberry jam, and the third vanilla buttercream.

7. You should now have a 10cm high cake. Place a cake board on top of the cake, and check if the cake is level with a spirit level. Gently press down on top of the cake to level it and to help it settle. This will help to ensure it doesn't spring back after covering and cause bulges.

TRIMMING

You now need to trim the sides of the cake so they are even and straight.

1. Place the cake on its board on the turntable. I usually place a cakeboard on top of the cake, so I can lean my hand on it while trimming the sides.

2. Hold your long sharp knife at a right angle to the turntable and cut downwards all around, trimming the sides of the cake until it is about 3mm smaller than the cake board, and the sides are straight.

3. Check the sides are straight by placing a set square against base board and rotating the turntable.

UNDERCOATING

To get a smooth, professional finish, you'll need a layer of either marzipan or ganache underneath your final coating of sugarpaste. This acts as a foundation layer, holding in all the bulges. Marzipan is traditionally used with fruit cakes, but can be used with sponge as well. However, I generally prefer chocolate ganache with sponge cakes. It gives a deep, rich flavour and can be smoothed into lovely straight sides with sharp top edges. It sets firm, which gives you a great surface for your final sugarpaste covering.

Undercoating with chocolate ganache

I usually start making the ganache before torting and filling the cake, as it needs to sit and thicken for two hours before using. It works best on a very cold or slightly frozen cake, so whilst you're making your ganache, put your cake in the freezer for about 20 minutes.

1. Make your ganache as per the recipe on p. 19.

2. Take a workboard around 10cm larger than the cake (I use a square piece of Perspex). Lay some greaseproof paper on your table, place the workboard on top, and tape the ends of the paper on the back, making sure the paper is taut with no creases.

3. Place your greaseproof covered workboard on a turntable, ideally with some non-stick matting underneath to keep it in place.

4. Place the semi-frozen cake on the workboard and draw around the cake board.

5. Remove the cake and spread a layer of ganache around 4mm thick on the circle you've just drawn.

6. Turn the cake upside down and place it so the top is on the ganache. Use a spirit level and press down on the cake to make sure it is level and well stuck to the ganache. It will stick quickly if you use a semi-frozen cake, otherwise leave for a few minutes to stick well.

7. Scrape the remaining ganache up the sides of the cake.

8. Using your angled spatula, cover the cake with ganache. Try to keep the underneath of the cake card clean, (this is on the top at the moment), as this will eventually sit on top of another cake.

9. Using a bench scraper, or any rectangular scraper, scrape the excess ganache off. Keep the scraper perpendicular to the turntable, and using the top cake card as a guide, spin the turntable with one hand, scraping off the excess. The scraper should be pressed down on the workboard and against the cake.

10. Add more ganache if needed and then scrape again. When you're happy, place in the freezer for 10 minutes.

11. Take out of the freezer, turn the right way up and carefully remove the greaseproof paper. There may be small dents on the top and/or sides, which you can fill in and scrape over again with ganache. If you are doing lots of tiers, you may need to warm up the ganache in the microwave. Do this in 15 second bursts, stirring in between, as chocolate burns very easily.

12. Place a metal spatula or scraper in hot water for a few minutes to heat up. Dry it off and then gently scrape over the top and sides of the cake one more time. This will neaten up any overhanging edges or odd sticky-out bits, especially around the top edge.

13. Leave your freshly ganached cake overnight to firm up.

Masking with Buttercream

If you're using an undercoat of marzipan on a sponge cake you'll also need to mask (or crumb coat) the cake with a thin coat of buttercream first. This traps all the errant crumbs as well as helping to seal in moisture and acting as a glue for the marzipan.

1. Use your offset spatula to apply a layer of buttercream to the top and sides of your cake. Don't worry at this stage if it's too thick, it's just important that all the cake is covered.

2. Hold the spatula or a small side scraper at a right angle to the turntable. Spin the turntable with one hand, scraping off the excess with the other.

3. Use the spatula to scrape the excess off the top. The buttercream should be thin enough to see the cake underneath

Undercoating with Marzipan

Marzipan is an almond paste which provides a lovely smooth undercoat, and will help to give your final layer of sugarpaste a smooth, professional finish. Try to buy white or natural coloured marzipan as this is usually the best quality.

1. For a fruit cake, brush boiled apricot jam over the cake to act as a glue for the marzipan. Fill in any dents on the cake with small pieces of marzipan. For a sponge cake, mask your cake with buttercream (see above) before starting.

2. Knead the marzipan until its soft and pliable. Don't over-knead as it will dry out and crack.

3. Measure the top and sides of the cake. For a 20cm cake with 10cm high sides, you will have to roll out a circle at least 40cm in diameter. It's best to roll out with a couple of extra inches, so I'd advise rolling the marzipan out to around 60cm.

4. Dust your work surface with icing sugar. Then, resting your rolling pin on the spacers, roll out the marzipan, turning it after each roll and adding more icing sugar if needed to make sure it doesn't stick. The spacers will ensure you roll out evenly. Keep rolling until the rolling pin starts sliding on the

spacers. This should give you a finished depth of around 4mm.

5. Fold the marzipan over the rolling pin, and drape over the cake. Smooth out the top first with the smoother, making sure no air is trapped, then work your way down the sides of the cake. Keep gently pulling out the 'skirt' of marzipan so you don't get creases.

6. Press one smoother at right angles to the baseboard and into the base of the cake to create a line to cut off the excess marzipan. Use both the smoothers to get a really clean finish.

7. To achieve a straight side and sharp edge, place one smoother on top and the other on the side, forming a right angle. Placing a firm pressure on your smoothers, gently smooth the marzipan on the side upwards, whilst simultaneously smoothing the marzipan on the top across to meet at the edge. Leave to firm up overnight.

COVERING WITH SUGARPASTE

Covering with sugarpaste is exactly the same process as covering with marzipan, but for this you'll have to work quite quickly, otherwise the sugarpaste will dry out. If you are colouring your sugarpaste, do this the day before and wrap in a plastic bag so that it has time to settle and the colour has time to fully develop. See p. 20 for sugarpaste recipes.

1. Brush all over your ganache or marzipan undercoated cake either with cooled boiled water, or with vodka. This acts as a glue for the sugarpaste. Make sure you don't leave any dry gaps, as they will cause air pockets.

2. Dust your work surface with icing sugar if you are covering a marzipan undercoat, or cornflour if you are covering a ganache undercoat.

3. Knead your sugarpaste until its pliable, trying not to trap any air bubbles in the sugarpaste. Don't over-knead as it will dry out and crack.

4. Resting your rolling pin on the spacers, roll out the sugarpaste, turning it after each roll, and adding more icing sugar if needed to make sure it doesn't stick. The spacers will ensure you roll out evenly. Keep rolling until the rolling pin starts sliding on the spacers. You should have an even depth of 4mm.

5. Fold the sugarpaste over the rolling pin and drape over the cake. Smooth out the top first with the smoother, making sure no air is trapped. Then work your way down the sides of the cake. Keep gently pulling out the 'skirt' of sugarpaste so you don't get creases.

6. Press one smoother at right angles to the baseboard and into the base of the cake to create a line to cut off the excess sugarpaste. Use both the smoothers to get a really smooth finish.

7. To achieve a straight side and sharp edge, place one smoother on top and the other on the side, forming a right angle. Placing a firm pressure on your smoothers, gently smooth the sugarpaste on the side upwards, whilst simultaneously smoothing the sugarpaste on the top across to meet at the edge. Leave to firm up overnight.

Covering the base drum
It's best to do this a few days before, so it has time to dry and firm up.

1. Use a 12mm high cake drum for the baseboard, making sure it is at least 5cm (2") larger than the biggest cake. Brush cooled boiled water all over the board.

2. Roll out enough sugarpaste to cover the cake drum at a thickness of 4mm. Place on the cake drum and smooth with a smoother.

3. Hold a knife at right angles to the board, and using the side of the board as a guide, trim the excess sugarpaste off.

COVERING EXTENDED HEIGHT TIERS

Your design may call for an extra high tier (a 20cm cake instead of a 10cm high cake). These are a little bit trickier to handle. It's best to use a ganache undercoat which gives you a sturdier structure.

1. Start by baking double your normal recipe, so you have four cakes instead of two.

2. Level, torte and fill as normal, so you have two 10cm high cakes, each on their own cake board.

3. Cover the top of the first cake with ganache and let this firm up.

4. Place the second cake on top, attaching it with a small bit of ganache on the board.

5. Now ganache the extra high cake as if it were one cake, and leave to firm up overnight.

6. Cover the tall tier as normal using one giant piece of sugarpaste, making sure you work quickly, so the extra weight of the sugarpaste doesn't tear.

7. Alternatively, it's often easier to cover the tall tier using two separate pieces of sugarpaste.
   • Cover the top with a cut out circle of sugarpaste the same size as the cake.
   • Measure the circumference and the height of the cake. Cut out a rectangle to these measurements, and carefully wrap around the cake. Smooth as usual. You will need to cover the join at the back and top with some flowers or a piped design.

Quantities of sugarpaste or marzipan needed to cover cakes

Cake Size	Size	Amount required	Covering the base drum
Round 10cm high	15cm	1000g	500g
	17.5cm	1250g	600g
	20cm	1800g	700g
	22.5cm	1750g	900g
	25cm	2250g	1000g
	27.5cm	2500g	1250g
	30cm	2750g	1500g
	32.5cm	3000g	1750g
	35cm	3500g	2000g

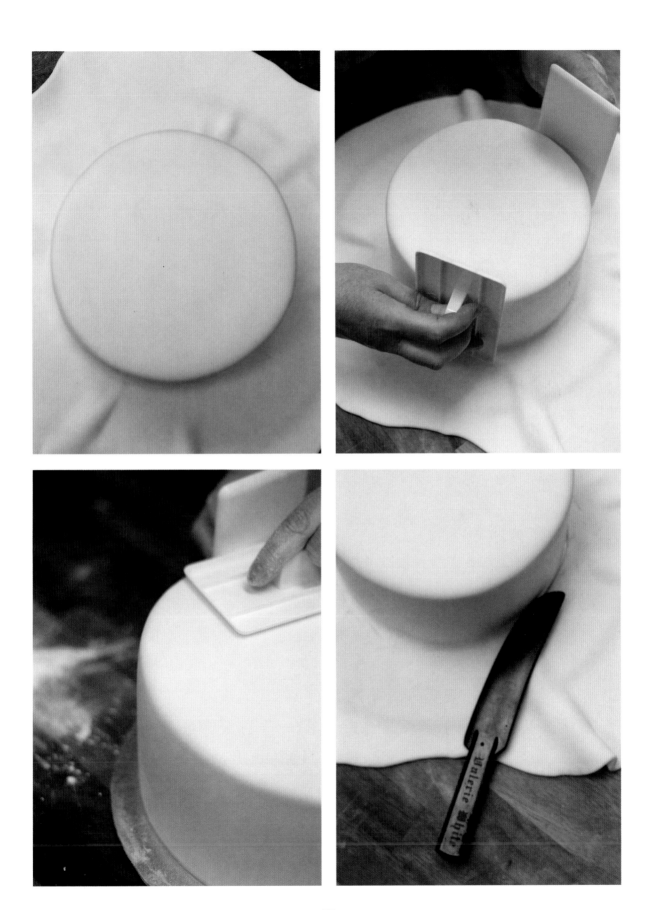

Stacking the Cake

DOWELLING THE CAKES

Each tier that has a cake resting on top of it will need to have dowels inserted to support the weight of the tier/s above.

Size of cake	Number of dowels
15cm	3
20cm and 22.5cm	4
25cm	6
30cm	7

The example below describes how to dowel an 20cm cake with a 15cm cake stacked on top.

1. Place a 15cm cake board on top of the 20cm cake and make a mark with a cocktail stick around the cake board.

2. Insert four plastic dowels just inside this mark. Make sure you insert them straight and push them all the way down until they hit the baseboard.

3. Using an edible ink pen, make a mark on each dowel, just very slightly above where they stick out from the cake.

4. Remove all the dowels and line them up so the ends are level. Find the highest mark, and draw a line straight across all the dowels.

5. Using a pair of garden secateurs (kept especially for this purpose), cut each dowel at this new mark. They should all be exactly the same height.

6. Wipe each dowel with vodka to sterilise them, then insert back into the cake.

7. Repeat for each tier except the top tier.

STACKING THE CAKES

1. Spread some royal icing over your previously covered and dried base drum.

2. Using a large palette knife, carefully lift the base tier (which is still on its own board) and place centrally on the base drum.

3. Pipe a large dot of royal icing over the top of each dowel, then carefully place the next tier centrally on top.

4. Repeat until you have finished stacking each tier.

Tools for covering the cake

1. Smoother
2. Pastry brush
3. Non-stick rolling pin
4. Non-stick rolling pin
5. Cake board
6. Cake drum
7. Turntable
8. Small icing sugar sifter
9. Toothpicks
10. Tape measure
11. Cake leveller
12. Spacers
13. Plastic dowels
14. Stainless steel ruler
15. Spirit level
16. Large offset spatula
17. Large sharp knife
18. Small spatula
19. Garden secateurs (to be only used for cutting your cake dowels – not your roses!)
20. Right-angled smoother
21. Scraper

General flowermaking tips

If you can't find big rose petal cutters, use heart or circle shaped cookie cutters

To make a cornflour dusting pouch, take a square of muslin, fill the center with cornflour, bring the ends together and tie an elastic band to secure.

Use a polystyrene cake dummy to stick wires in when drying smaller flowers

It's often advisable to assemble complicated things like a top-tier bouquet, once the cake is in situ at the wedding venue. If a breakage occurs, it needn't be a disaster. For smaller flowers, simply remove the flower and scrape off any royal icing. For a larger flower (in the bouquet, for example) gently break off the damaged petals. The overall look of the flower should remain intact.

Use cardboard or polystyrene apple and fruit trays to dry larger petals and flowers in. Their curved surfaces will give your flowers a rounded shape. Dry smaller unwired blossoms in the indents of 'dimple foam' available from decorating suppliers.

To store flowers for longer periods (or to preserve the bouquet after the wedding), keep them in a cardboard box, with a sachet of silica gel to absorb the moisture. The cardboard will allow the air to get to it and keep it dry and moisture-free.

Use double sided tape to attach 15mm ribbon around the edge of the cake drum. This gives a neat, professional finish.

You can make rose centres using modelling paste. Just make sure these are made a few days in advance so they are dry when you come to use them. These will be heavier than polystyrene balls.

Coloured sugarpaste requires a lot of kneading to mix in the colour evenly. Do this a day ahead as the paste can get very warm and too soft to use straight away. This will also allow time for the colour to develop.

When cutting petals, make sure you rub the cutter on your worksurface (I use a high density plastic chopping board), then lift up the cutter with the paste still in and rub your finger over the edges, or rub a small rolling pin over the back of the cutter to help get rid of any furry edges.

Store flowerpaste shapes inside a plastic folder until you're ready to use them. This will stop them drying out in the process.

Decoration and flower making tools and equipment

1. Non-stick board
2. Small non-stick rolling pin
3. Tiny non-stick rolling pin
4. Wires
5. Needle nose pliers
6. Wire cutters
7. White pearl dust
8. Cream pearl dust
9. Gold dust
10. Gold paint
11. Coloured dusts
12. Piping bag
13. Large blossom cutter and veiner
14. Hydrangea cutter and veiner
15. Flower, leaf and geometric cutters
16. Flower centre moulds
17. Piping nozzles
18. Peony cutters
19. Rose petal cutter
20. Rose cutters
21. Tiny blossom plunger cutters
22. Dimple foam
23. Paste colours
24. Toothpicks
25. Edible glue
26. Paintbrushes
27. Posy picks
28. Veiner
29. Ball tool and other modelling tools
30. Floral tape
31. Small offset spatula
32. Scriber
33. Scalpel
34. Small scissors
35. Cornflour dusting pouch
36. Firm foam pad
37. Apple tray

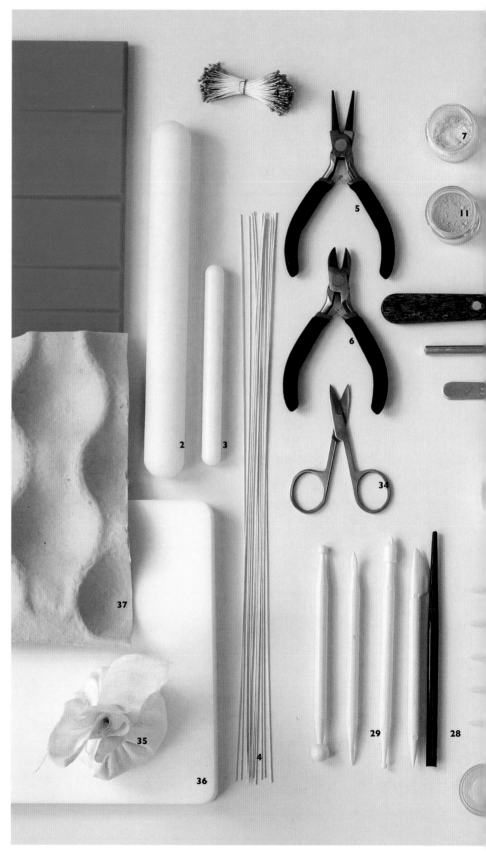

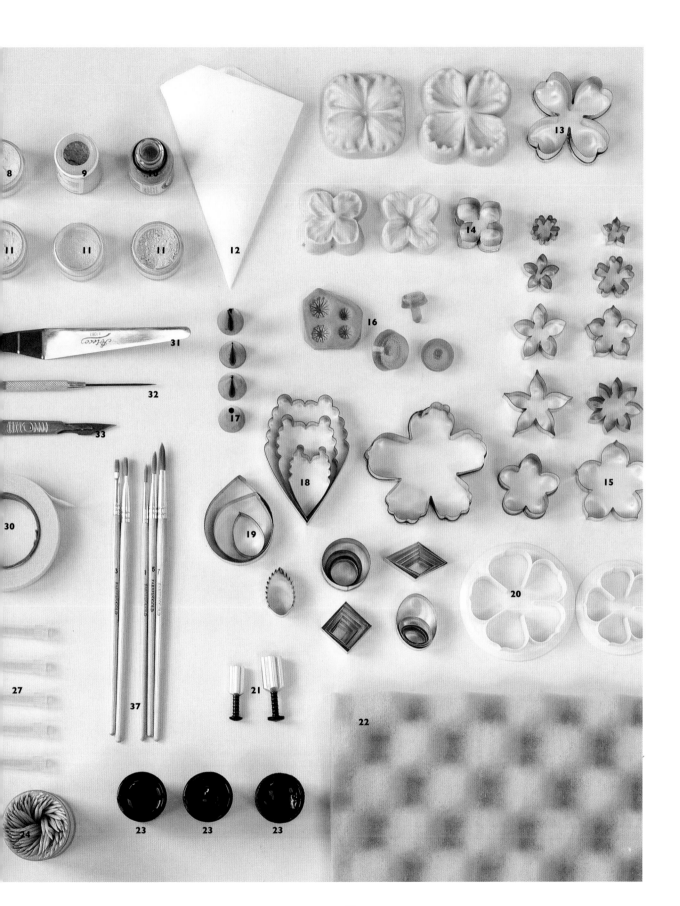

PEPPERMINT SCROLLS

I was asked to create a cake for a wedding, which was taking place in the Terrace Room at Grove House, Roehampton College. Inspired by the wonderful Georgian mouldings and panels on the walls, I decided to make a cake that had the delicate vintage feel of traditional royal iced and piped cakes, yet still managed to be fresh and contemporary.

Although the design may look complicated, a lot of the detail is easily achieved using moulds or cutters. The trickiest part is creating the frills, but you can practice making these first until you're happy with them.

How To Make It

Techniques used

/ Using moulds
/ Dusting with lustre dust
/ Painting with metallic edible paint
/ Cutter leaves
/ Creating frills
/ Making a frilled topper
/ Flower paste twisted ribbons

Equipment needed

/ Tiny leaf cutter
/ Cream flower paste
/ Edible glue (see p. 23)
/ Ivory sugarpaste
/ Edible silver paint
/ Pearl lustre dust
/ Pale green lustre dust
/ Cornflour dusting pouch (see p. 43)
/ Firm foam pad
/ Stitching wheel
/ Scalpel
/ Steel ruler
/ 60mm polystyrene ball
/ No. 18 florist's wire
/ Hot glue gun
/ Feather mould
/ Cameo mould
/ Ball tool
/ Tape measure
/ Small non-stick rolling pin
/ Cocktail sticks
/ Small paintbrush

FOR YOUR BASE STRUCTURE

Start with

- 1 x 25cm x 10cm cake
- 1 x 20cm x 10cm cake
- 1 x 15cm x 15cm cake
- 1 x 10cm x 5cm cake
- 1 x 30cm cake drum

1. Cover the tiers and the cake drum in pale mint green sugarpaste. This cake calls for coloured sugarpaste, which requires a lot of kneading to mix in the colour. Do this a day ahead as the paste can get very warm and too soft to use straight away. This will also allow time for the colour to develop.

2. Dowel and stack your cakes.

TOP TIER FEATHERS

3. Knead equal amounts of ivory sugarpaste and cream flower paste together. Take a small amount of this mixture and place in the feather silcone mould. Spread it right out to the edges but make sure to keep all the paste inside the mould. Flex the mould and release. Make 20 of these.

4. Paint edible glue on the top two thirds of the back of a feather and attach to the top tier, folding the very top of the feather onto the top of the cake, and slightly curling the bottom edge of the feather up with your finger. Repeat for all the feathers.

RIBBON SCROLLS

5. Roll out strips of cream flower paste quite thinly.

6. Using the steel ruler and scalpel, cut neat ribbons 1.5cm x 60cm for the top tier, 1.5cm x 75cm for the third tier and 1.5cm x 110cm for the second tier. Don't worry if you can't cut one single strip long enough, as you can always overlap multiple strips when you're attaching them to the cake.

7. Paint edible glue on the very bottom edge of the top tier.

8. Twist the strip and carefully place around the cake. Repeat at the bases of the two middle tiers.

FRILLS

9. Roll out another piece of flower paste and using the steel ruler and scalpel, cut three neat ribbons of 2.5cm x 30cm.

10. Place two cocktail sticks across the ribbon at 3cm and 6cm from the end.

11. Use the cocktail sticks to bring the flower paste ribbon together so it rises up and creates a gentle fold.

12. Now take the first cocktail stick and place it 3cm away from the second cocktail stick. Repeat steps 10 and 11 until the whole strip is folded in a concertina fashion.

13. Gently run the stitching wheel lengthwise along the centre of the frills. Make sure not to press too hard, or the frill will fall apart when you try to attach it to the cake.

14. Paint a line of glue around the middle of the double height 15cm tier, and attach the three frills all around the cake, overlapping the ends of each one so the joins are not visible. Apply gently with fingers so as not to squash the frill, and hold for about 10 seconds at each section to ensure it is stuck.

15. Repeat steps 10-14 using six ribbons of flower paste 3cm x 30cm. Apply this frill to the base of the bottom tier.

CAMEOS

16. Mix equal amounts of sugarpaste and flower paste together. Put a small ball of this into the cameo mould and push it out to the edges with your fingers. Make sure to keep all the paste inside the mould. Make four cameos.

17. Dust the background with pale green lustre dust and dust the face with pearl lustre dust.

18. Paint the metallic frame with edible silver paint. You can either buy readymade paint, or mix silver lustre dust with a few drops of vodka to make your own.

19. Glue the cameos to the second tier cake at four equal measurements.

RIBBONS AND BOWS

20. Cut four strips of thinly rolled cream flower paste 1.5cm x 6cm. Fold over the ends to the centre to form a bow and glue.

21. Cut a small strip of flower paste 1.5cm x 2.5cm, and paint edible glue on the back. Then fold it over the join in the middle of the bow. Set aside to dry a little.

22. Paint a line of edible glue on the cake in sweeping curves between the cameos on the second tier. Twist some long 1.5cm-wide strips and attach to the cake on the glued curves.

23. Take some more twisted strips and trim the ends at a 45 degree angle. Glue these on either side of each cameo. Finally, glue on the bow.

LEAVES

24. Using a tiny leaf cutter, cut out leaves from thinly rolled cream flower paste and use the small ball tool on the firm foam pad to gently curve the leaves. Glue to the top edge of the base tier with each leaf alternately pointing upwards and downwards.

FRILLED BALL ORNAMENT

25. Take a 60mm polystyrene ball and attach a 10cm length of no. 18 florist's wire to it.

26. Roll out more cream flower paste and cut it in 5cm x 10cm strips. Fold these in half lengthwise and pinch together at the fold to form a ruffle.

27. Glue these all over the polystyrene ball, and glue a strip of flower paste over the wire.

28. Push a posy pick (see right) containing a small amount of modelling paste into the centre of the top tier and insert the wire into this.

29. Glue another bow and tails to the wire.

USING A POSY PICK
You must never insert wired flowers or large decorations directly into a cake in case they rust. Instead, use a small, pointed plastic container called a 'posy pick'. Insert the wires into the posy pick and then push a small ball of sugarpaste or pipe some royal icing into the base to help secure the wires and stop the bouquet or decoration moving.

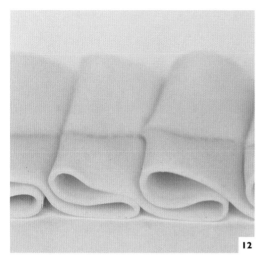

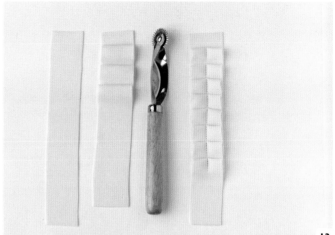

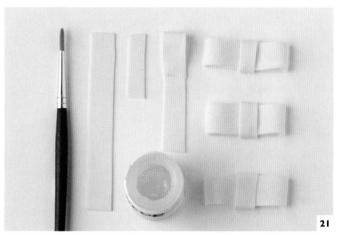

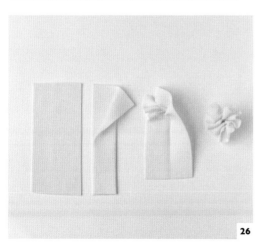

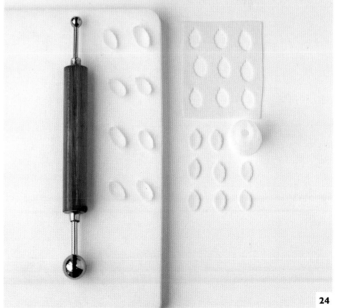

PEONIES
AND
RIBBONS

A simple three-tier cake with deep pink peonies and a stylish pleated satin ribbon.

Peonies are a perennially popular flower for weddings – less traditional than a rose, but with the drama of multiple petals and rich colours. Unfortunately, they are only available in spring and summer, and don't last too well out of water. Sugar peonies make a beautiful substitute for the real flowers. On this cake I made them extra opulent with gold stamens and a dusting of lustrous gold on the petals.

How To Make It

Techniques used

/ Making closed peonies

/ Making open peonies

/ Dusting with gold lustre dust

/ Using stamens

/ Attaching ribbons

Equipment needed

/ Royal icing (see p. 24)

/ No. 2 piping tip

/ Paper piping bag (see p. 24)

/ 1m x 5cm ivory satin pleated ribbon

/ 1m x 3mm ivory grosgrain ribbon

/ 1.3m x 15mm ivory grosgrain ribbon

FOR YOUR BASE STRUCTURE

Start with

•1 x 25cm x 10cm cake

•1 x 20cm x 10cm cake

•1 x 15cm x 10cm cake

•1 x 30cm cake drum

1. Cover all the tiers and cake drum with ivory sugarpaste. Leave overnight to dry.

2. The next day, dowel and stack your cakes.

FLOWERS

3. Following the instructions on p. 68, make 18 large closed peonies and three smaller closed peonies using dark pink flower paste. Dust the edges of the petals with gold lustre dust.

4. Following the instructions on p. 64, make eight dark pink open peonies.

ATTACHING THE FLOWERS

5. Take a large closed peony and cut off the wire close to the base. Pipe a large dot of quite stiff royal icing on the top tier and carefully press the peony onto this. Do this for two more, arranging them so they are facing outwards and the backs of each flower are touching.

6. Fill in the gaps between these first three with the small closed peonies, attaching them with more large dots of royal icing.

7. Attach the eight open peonies on the ledge between the top and middle tier using royal icing as above.

8. Attach the 15 large closed peonies on the ledge between the middle and base tier using royal icing as above.

ATTACHING THE RIBBON

9. Wrap the pleated ribbon around the base tier and cut to size, leaving a small overlap. Attach this with a few dots of royal icing, making sure the join is at the back.

10. Tie the thin 3mm ribbon with a small bow centrally over the pleated ribbon.

11. Attach the 15mm ivory grosgrain ribbon around the drum using double-sided sticky tape.

Open Peony

Equipment needed

- / Florist's tape
- / Dark pink flower paste
- / Edible gold lustre dust
- / Gold stamens
- / Edible glue (see p. 23)
- / Firm foam pad
- / Ball tool
- / Small non-stick rolling pin
- / Small paintbrush for glue
- / Hollyhock cutter in two sizes, 85mm and 75mm
- / 80mm two-part veining set

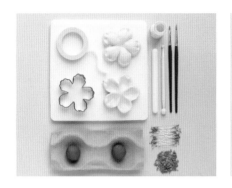

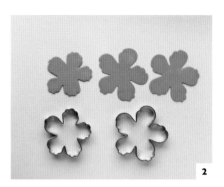

1

2

3

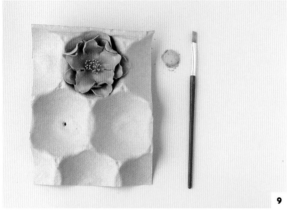

9

8

5

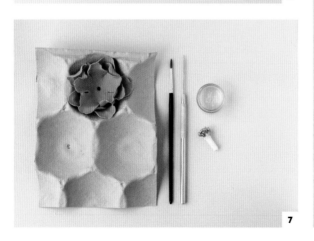

7

1. Colour the flower paste a dark pink

2. Thinly roll out the dark pink flower paste and cut out two shapes with the smaller hollyhock cutter (you could also use a five-petal rose cutter) and one with the larger cutter.

3. Press each shape between the two-part veiner to vein and shape.

4. Place on the firm foam pad and use the ball tool to thin out and gently frill the edges. Then leave to dry in a curved apple tray until the pieces are leather hard (half an hour or so).

5. Take around 20 gold-tipped stamens and tape together with the florist's tape. Trim the ends so the stamens measure 2cm long.

6. Make a hole in the centre of one of the indents in the apple tray large enough to fit the bunch of stamens.

7. Place the large hollyhock shape into this and brush a dab of glue in the centre. Place a smaller hollyhock shape onto this, making sure the petals are overlapping, and then repeat for the third shape.

8. Poke a hole in the centre of the flower with the end of a paintbrush. Brush glue onto the taped end of the stamens and push them through this hole and the hole in the apple tray. Then leave to dry.

9. Brush the centre and edges of each petal with edible gold lustre dust.

Wired Closed Peony

Equipment needed

- / No. 18 florist's wire
- / No. 26 florist's wire
- / Hot glue gun
- / Florist's tape
- / Dark pink flower paste
- / Edible gold lustre dust
- / Edible glue (see p. 23)
- / 25mm polystyrene ball
- / Firm foam pad
- / Ball tool
- / Small non-stick rolling pin
- / Small paintbrush for glue
- / Veining tool
- / Set of three peony cutters
- / 80mm hollyhock cutter and veining set

3

5

6

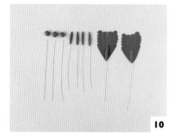

10

9

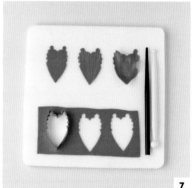

6

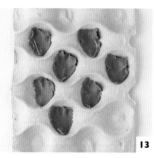

13

7

9

14

15

FLOWER CENTRE AND INNER PETALS

1. Cut a length of no. 18 wire into three equal lengths, and using a hot glue gun, glue a wire into the polystyrene ball to form the centre of the peony.

2. Thinly roll out the dark pink flower paste and cut two shapes using a five-petal cutter. Here I use a hollyhock cutter, but you could also use a five-petal rose cutter.

3. Place one shape between the two-part veiner and press firmly. Then, on the firm foam pad, gently rub the ball tool along the edges of the petals to thin them out and give them some movement.

4. Place in the indent of an apple tray and leave to dry until it's leather hard. This usually takes around half an hour. Then repeat for the second shape.

5. Take one shape and brush edible glue about two thirds of the way up each petal. Thread the wire through the centre of the petal shape and attach the petals to the polystyrene ball, overlapping them as you go. Make sure you cover the ball with the petals so no polystyrene is showing.

6. Take the second partially dried shape and brush edible glue about two thirds of the way up each petal. Thread the wire through the centre of this shape and again attach the petals to the ball in such a way that they overlap, leaving a small gap between the first layer of petals and this layer.

MIDDLE PETAL LAYERS

7. Cut out five petals using the medium-sized peony petal cutter. With the petal on your workboard, roll the veining tool to impress veins on each petal.

8. Place each petal on the firm foam pad and thin out the edges using the ball tool. Then place in an apple tray and leave to dry for about half an hour until they are leather hard.

9. Paint edible glue about halfway up from the base of each petal, and then attach them to the flower, overlapping each one. Leave to dry hanging upside down (see right).

WIRED OUTER PETALS

10. Cut a length of no. 26 florist's wire into four equal lengths. Dip the end of one piece of wire into the edible glue, and then push it into a tiny ball of pink flower paste, rolling the paste between your thumb and forefinger into a thin oblong shape and pushing it about 2cm down the wire. Repeat for all pieces of wire.

11. Cut five petals using the large peony cutter. Paint edible glue in a line centrally about 2cm up from the base of one petal. Place one of the wires with the paste on the glue and press it firmly to attach.

12. Now carefully vein the petal with the veining tool. Make sure you work either side of the glued wire. Place on the firm foam and thin out the edges of the petal using the ball tool.

13. Repeat for each petal, then place in an apple tray and leave to dry overnight.

ASSEMBLING THE OUTER PETALS

14. Take a 10cm length of florist's tape and stretch it to release the glue. Then, holding the peony upside down, wrap the florist's tape once around the wire close to the base of the flower. Keep wrapping round the wire, incorporating and taping each wire of the large outer petals to the main wire, making sure each petal overlaps the previous.

15. Brush the edges of each petal with edible gold lustre dust.

> **TIP FOR DRYING WIRED FLOWERS**
> Make an impromptu flower-drying stand by resting a wire oven shelf on two mugs. Then make a hook at the end of the flower wire and hook this on the wire shelf. This way your flowers dry upside down, and the petals are more likely to stay in shape.

VINTAGE
HAT BOXES

For the bride who loves hats!
I used pastel coloured vintage hatboxes as
inspiration for this cake, and decorated it
with an extravagant fabric-like sugar bow
and piped decorations. People are often
scared of piping, but it's really quite easy
– just make sure you practice on a piece of
paper or a cake dummy first, until you get
your confidence up.

How To Make It

Techniques used

/ Wrapping an extra layer of paste to create a box lid

/ Piping; dots, leaves, pressure piped blossoms

/ Painting on cakes

/ Embossing modelling paste to make a fabric texture

Equipment needed

/ Edible glue (see p. 23)

/ Edible gold paint

/ Cornflour dusting pouch (see p. 43)

/ Small square-ended paintbrush

/ Measuring tape

/ Pizza cutter

/ Paste food colour

/ Cream flower paste

/ Ridged roller

/ No. 1.5 piping nozzle

/ No. 51 medium leaf piping nozzle

/ 15mm ivory grosgrain ribbon

FOR YOUR BASE STRUCTURE

Start with

- 1 x 23cm x 15cm cake (peach tier)
- 1 x 20cm x 17.5cm cake (mint green tier)
- 1 x 17.5cm x 10cm cake (pink tier)
- 1 x 15cm x 10cm cake (pale blue tier)
- 1 x 28cm cake drum

1. Colour the sugarpaste for each tier, making the following quantities:
   - 2.5kg peach sugarpaste
   - 2kg mint green sugarpaste
   - 1.2kg pink sugarpaste
   - 1kg pale blue sugarpaste

   To achieve vintage looking colours, add a tiny speck of black food colour to your main colour.

2. Wrap each colour in a plastic bag and leave to rest overnight so the paste is not too soft to use.

3. Cover each tier as specified above, and cover the cake drum with the peach sugarpaste. Leave overnight to dry. You should have plenty of sugarpaste left over. Wrap this up and put it to one side.

LIDS

For the peach coloured tier (tier 1)

4. Knead a teaspoon of Tylose powder into the remaining peach sugarpaste, wrap well in clingfilm and leave to strengthen for half an hour. (Please note, the images here show the technique as used for the top, blue tier).

5. Cut a strip of baking paper 90cm x 6cm and wrap this around the base of the cake. The top edge will act as a guide so you can place the lid strip in a straight line.

6. Roll out some of the strengthened paste until it's 4mm thick. Then, using your pizza cutter, cut a strip 90cm x 9cm. Roll this strip up carefully.

7. Brush sugar glue on the top 9cm of the tier and carefully unroll the paste strip onto this, keeping the top edge level with the top of the cake.

8. Overlap the end, and cut through both layers. Take the excess away and smooth over the join.

For the remaining tiers

9. Repeat steps 4-8 for the other tiers, cutting and gluing paste strips in matching colours to the following dimensions:
   - Mint green tier (tier 2): 80cm x 5cm.
   - Pink tier (tier 3): 60cm x 5cm.
   - Pale blue tier (tier 4): 50cm x 5cm.

GOLD LINES

10. Using a small square-end brush, paint the gold lines on the top and base of each lid. You can use readymade edible paint or make your own by mixing gold lustre dust with a few drops of vodka. If you place the cake on a turntable, you can steady your arm on the edge of the turntable and then rotate it, keeping the brush still.

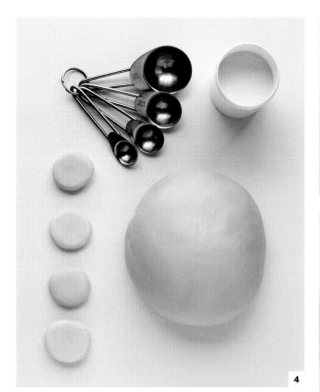

4

6

7a

10

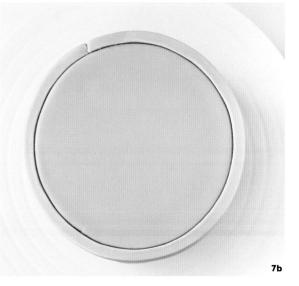

7b

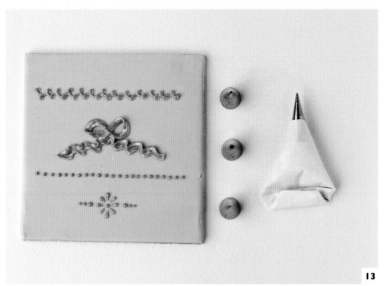

13

13a

13b

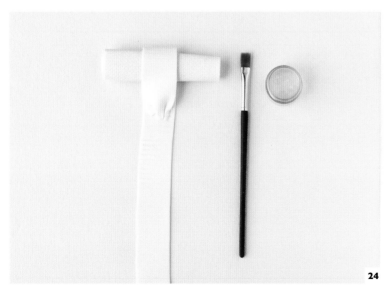

25

13c

24

22

PIPING

11. Make up one amount of royal icing (see p. 24) and colour it with the shade 'Autumn Leaf'.

12. Put four teaspoons of the icing inside your piping bag (see p. 24). Place a damp cloth over the bowl with the remaining icing, so it doesn't dry out.

13. Practice the following techniques on paper until you're confident enough to do them on the cakes:
    * *Leaves*: Using a no. 1.5 piping nozzle, pipe a small dot. Then, without releasing the tip from the dot, stop squeezing and pull the tip through the piped dot and away to create a 'tail'.
    * *Leaf garlands*: Pipe one comma shaped leaf as above pointing upwards, and the next pointing downwards.
    * *Floral designs*: Pipe a dot, then using the same technique as the leaves, pipe eight 'petals' pointing in towards the dot. Pipe three dots on either side of the flower.
    * *Bows and ribbon tails*: Use a no. 51 'medium leaf tip' nozzle to pipe a sideways figure 8 for the bow. Then pipe the ribbon tails using a gentle zig zag motion.

14. *For the peach tier (tier 1)*: Using a toothpick, mark dots at eight even intervals around the centre of the lid, and pipe floral designs at these points. Pipe leaf garlands just above and below the lines you painted in step 10.

15. *For the mint green tier (tier 2)*: Using a toothpick, mark eight points at even intervals around the tier, 6cm up from the base, and pipe bows and ribbon tails at these points.

16. *For the pink tier (tier 3)*: Pipe a leaf garland just below the painted line. Then mark eight points at even intervals around the lid towards the bottom painted line and pipe small floral designs and dots.

17. *For the pale blue tier (tier 4)*: Pipe leaf garlands just above and below the painted lines. Pipe a line of dots along the centre of the lid.

18. Leave all the icing to dry and then paint with edible gold paint.

ASSEMBLING THE TIERS

19. Dowel and stack the cakes.

20. Attach a length of 15mm ivory grosgrain ribbon to the base of each tier. Cut to 3cm longer than the circumference of the cake, and use a non-toxic glue stick to secure the overlap.

21. Using double-sided tape, attach a 15mm ribbon around the edge of the cake drum (base board) to give a neat, professional finish.

RIBBON BOW

22. Roll out some more cream flower paste to 2-3mm thick. Cut three strips measuring 40cm x 3cm. A pizza cutter is ideal for this as it won't tear the paste.

23. Roll the ridged roller along the length of each strip to emboss a ridged fabric-like texture into the paste.

24. To make the bow, cut one strip of the textured flower paste so it measures 25cm long. Paint some edible glue in the centre of this strip, then bring each end in to the centre to create two loops. Roll up some paper towel and place inside the loops to keep the open shape whilst the bow is drying. Leave to dry for an hour or two.

25. Cut a 6cm x 3cm strip of the textured flower paste and wrap around the centre of the bow, hiding the join. Glue this on the back of the bow.

26. While the bow is drying, cut the ends of the other two lengths of textured flower paste at a 45 degree angle to create the ribbon tails, which drape down the side of the cake.

27. Paint some glue on the top of the top tier and attach each ribbon tail. As you are arranging the ribbon tails on the side of the cake, slightly loop and twist them to give a natural draped feel. You may need to attach them with edible glue where they touch the cake.

28. Finally, glue the partly dried bow on the top tier over the ribbon tails.

BEES
AND
BLOSSOMS

This cake was created for a wedding that was held at the Royal Botanic Gardens at Kew and is covered in masses of flowers with tiny gold bees flying amongst them. There are a lot of sugar flowers on this design, but you can make them well in advance and store them in cardboard boxes with a packet of silica gel so they don't get damp and droopy.

This cake requires the use of moulds. You can buy them readymade, but it's really easy and fun to make your own – and it lends a personal touch to the cake. In this one I used a small bee charm, but you can use anything you like – brooches often work well – just make sure the object you are taking the mould from has a flattish back and that you can easily press it into the silicone putty.

How To Make It

Techniques used

- / Making and using moulds
- / Dusting with lustre dust
- / Making cutter flowers
- / Making wired peonies
- / Making wired jasmine and buds
- / Making wired blossoms
- / Making wired roses

Equipment needed

- / Ball tool
- / Firm foam pad
- / Dimple foam
- / Small paintbrush
- / Soft paintbrush for dusting
- / Edible glue (see p. 23)
- / Flower paste
- / Paste colours
- / Edible gold lustre dust
- / Dimple foam
- / Silicone mould putty
- / Bee charm (or similar)
- / Small non-stick rolling pin
- / Cornflour dusting pouch (see p. 43)
- / Floral tape
- / Large posy pick

FOR YOUR BASE STRUCTURE

Start with:

- 1 x 25cm x 10cm cake
- 1 x 20cm x 10cm cake
- 1 x 15cm x 10cm cake
- 1 x 10cm x 10cm cake
- 1 x 30cm (12") cake drum

1. Cover all the tiers and cake drum with ivory sugarpaste. Leave overnight to dry.

2. The next day, dowel and stack your cakes.

3. Attach a 15mm ivory grosgrain ribbon to the base of each tier and around the drum.

FLOWERS AND LEAVES

4. Colour the flower paste in five shades of pink, varying from very pale to darker pinks.

5. Following the instructions on p. 90 for cutter flowers, make groups of flowers in each shade of pink. So, for example, using the palest pink colour, make around 60 tiny flowers, 40 small flowers, 30 medium flowers and 20 large flowers. Repeat for each shade of flower paste.

6. Dust the centres of the blossoms with the gold lustre dust.

7. Following the instructions on p. 93, make 80 leaves in various sizes with the same pale green flower paste.

8. Attach the flowers and leaves to the sides of the cake. Start with the bigger flowers in each shade. Pipe a dot of royal icing on the ledges, then press the flower onto this for a few seconds to attach.

9. Continue by attaching the medium-sized flowers above and below, and finally fill in the gaps with the tiny flowers and the leaves. Work with one colour at a time.

10. Pipe small dots of icing in the centres of the tiny flowers.

GOLDEN BEES

11. Using a mould and yellow modelling paste, make 25 golden bees as described to the right, and dust with edible gold lustre dust.

12. Paint the backs of the bees with edible glue and attach to cake in between the flowers so that some are flying upwards and towards the flowers, some are on their own, and others are grouped together.

WIRED TOP TIER BOUQUET

13. Following the instructions on the indicated pages, make the following:
    • Two or three closed peonies (p. 68)
    • Two wired roses (p. 106)
    • Four or five stems of jasmine and buds (p. 102)
    • 12 small wired blossoms (p. 94)
    • 12 small wired hydrangea blossoms (p. 98)

14. Start with the larger flowers. Hold them upside down by their wires and tape together with the floral tape, then add in the jasmine and buds and the small blossoms. As the flowers can be very brittle when they're dry, I usually do this over a folded towel in case I drop any.

15. You can tape a few wires together at a time, and then cut the wires at the base at staggered lengths so the final stem doesn't become too thick.

16. To attach the bouquet to the cake, cut the wire stem to the correct length for your posy pick (see p. 54). Then insert the posy pick into the centre of the top tier and slot the bouquet into this. If you are transporting the cake, it may be safer to do this once the cake has been set up on the table

MAKING A MOULD

Equipment needed
• Two-part food safe silicon putty (often called Silicone Plastique)
• Small metal charm from a necklace or earring
• Edible gold lustre dust
• Modelling paste (see p. 20.)

How to make it
A. Wash and sterilise the metal charm in sterilising fluid.
B. Mix equal parts of the white and blue silicone putty together until an even blue colour is achieved. Then roll into a ball and flatten slightly.
C. Press the charm face down into the putty until it's level and leave to set as per the silicone putty instructions.
D. Once the mould has set, remove the charm and press a small ball of modelling paste into the mould cavity, making sure the paste is just flush with the edge of the mould.
E. Gently flex the mould to release the shape.

B

C

E

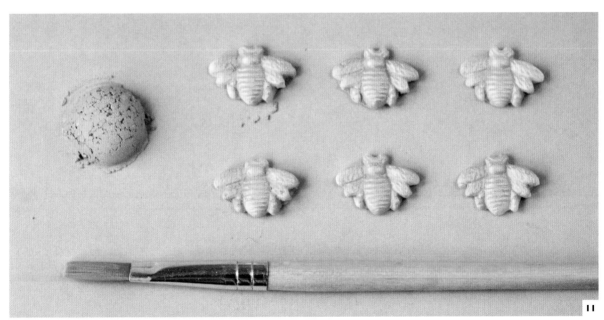

II

Cutter Flowers And Leaves

Equipment needed

/ Flower paste

/ Paste colours

/ Various metal or plastic flower cutters

/ Edible dusts

/ Dimple foam

/ Flower centres mould

/ Edible glue (see p. 23)

/ Firm foam pad

/ Ball tool

/ Small non-stick rolling pin

/ Small paintbrush for glue

/ Cornflour dusting pouch (see p. 43)

/ Knife modelling tool

3

4

8

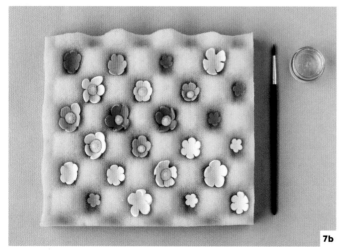

5

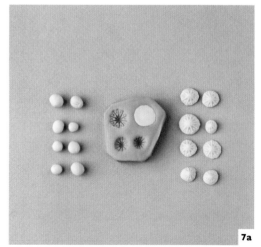

7b

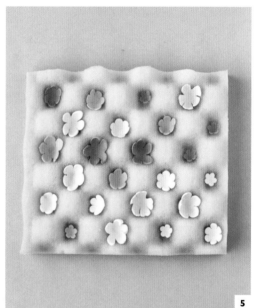

7a

PETALS

1. Colour the flower paste using paste colour. It's best to start with a tiny amount of colour as it's very concentrated, and you can always make it darker by adding more. Use a toothpick to transfer the colour.

2. Dust your work surface with a small amount of cornflour, and roll out your flower paste as thinly as possible (around 0.5mm, although for some flowers such as daisies with lots of delicate petals, you may need to leave it a bit thicker).

3. Cut out the shapes. When cutting, make sure you rub the cutter on your work surface (I use a high density plastic chopping board), then lift up the cutter with the paste still in and rub your finger over the edges or rub a small rolling pin over the back of the cutter to get rid of any jagged edges.

4. Place the cut out shape on the firm foam pad and use the ball tool to thin out the edges. Then place the flowers into the dimple foam so that they dry in a cupped shape.

5. For the smaller flowers you should use the ball tool after the shape has been placed in the dimple foam, and just use a round and round movement to thin and cup the flower.

6. Use a soft, flat-ended brush to gently dust the flowers with a tiny bit of edible dust colour, adding extra depth and dimension. Always wipe your brush on some kitchen paper to get rid of any excess before you dust the flower.

MOULDED CENTRE

7. Take a tiny ball of pale green or yellow paste and press it into the flower-centre mould, making sure it doesn't overlap the edges. Extract it and glue it into the centre of the flower with edible glue. Alternatively you can pipe a flower centre using royal icing, or glue a small sugar dragee in the centre.

LEAVES

8. Thinly roll out the pale green flower paste, and leave it to dry for five to ten minutes until it's leather hard. Cut a strip a bit wider than the leaf cutter.

9. Place the cutter on the paste and press firmly into the work surface, rubbing the cutter back and forwards. Hold one end of the cutter and tap the other end firmly to release the leaf from the cutter.

10. Use the knife modelling tool to make an indentation down the centre of the leaf. Then, place the cut out leaf on the firm foam pad and use the ball tool to thin out the edges and give it some curl and movement.

Small Wired Blossoms

Equipment needed

/ No. 24 florist's wire
/ Small scissors
/ Cream flower paste
/ Pale green flower paste
/ Edible glue (see p. 23)
/ Needle nose pliers
/ Pearl lustre dust
/ Pale pink dust
/ Cornflour dusting pouch (see p. 43)
/ Firm foam pad
/ Ball tool
/ Small non-stick rolling pin
/ Five-pointed modelling tool
/ Small paintbrush for glue
/ Soft paintbrush for dusting

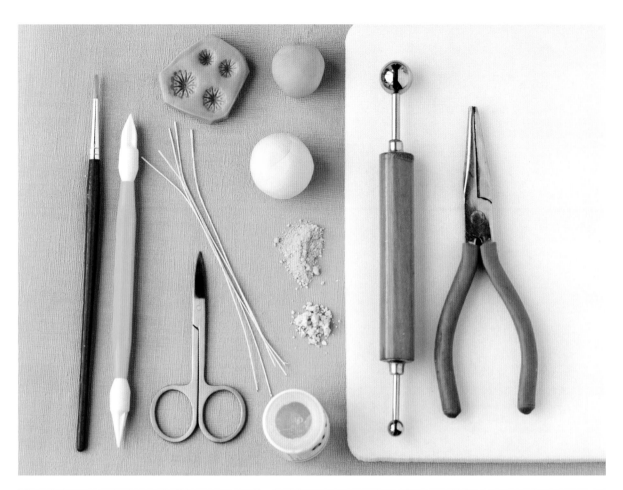

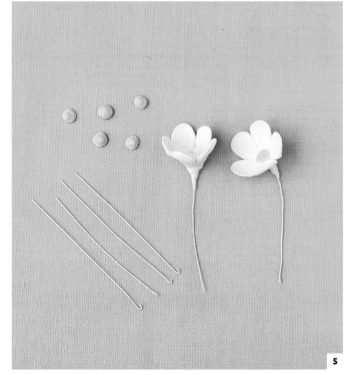

1. Take a small ball of flower paste and roll it into an elongated cone shape.

2. Take the five-pointed end of the modelling tool and press into the wider end of the cone, so you have five marks. Cut each mark down by about 1cm for the petals.

3. Press each petal outwards gently with your fingers and then place the flower on the firm foam and thin each petal out using the ball tool.

4. Cut each length of florist's wire into three equal lengths. Take one of the lengths and make a little hook at the end of it with your pliers.

5. Dip the hooked end into edible glue and thread it through the centre of the blossom, twisting the end of the cone onto the wire to make sure it's firmly attached. Take off any excess paste.

6. Make a centre for the blossom by pressing a tiny ball of pale green flower paste into the flower centre mould. Trim the excess, press it out of the mould and glue it to the centre of the flower with edible glue.

Wired Hydrangea Blossoms

Equipment needed

/ No. 26 florist's wire
/ Cream flower paste
/ Blue flower paste
/ Edible glue (see p. 23)
/ Needle nose pliers
/ Cornflour dusting pouch (see p. 43)
/ Firm foam pad
/ Ball tool
/ Small non-stick rolling pin
/ Small paintbrush for glue
/ Knife modelling tool
/ Veining tool
/ Hydrangea flower cutter

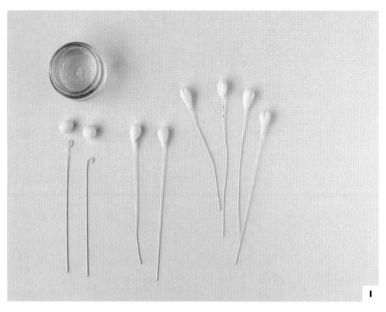

1

5

6

8

7

1. Cut each wire into four equal parts and make a hook in the end of each wire with the pliers.

2. Take a tiny piece of cream flower paste and roll it into a ball. Dip the hooked end of one of the wires into the edible glue and push it through the centre of the ball.

3. Twist the end of the paste ball so it is firmly attached to the wire, and pinch off any excess.

4. Using the knife modelling tool, make four indents from the top of the ball down the sides to form the centre of the flower. Leave to dry.

5. Thinly roll out some blue flower paste and cut it using the hydrangea flower cutter. Rub the cutter firmly into your workboard so you don't get furry edges.

6. Use the veining tool on your workboard to vein each petal. Then place on the firm foam pad and thin out the very edges of each petal using the ball tool.

7. Dab some edible glue on the bottom edge of the centre you made earlier, and then thread the wire through the centre of the blossom. Hold the blossom upside down and pinch the base to make sure it's firmly attached to the centre and the wire.

8. Bend the wire to dry the blossom upside down so the petals fall in a natural shape.

Wired Jasmine Blossoms and Buds

Equipment needed

/ No. 26 florist's wire
/ Pink flower paste
/ Green flower paste
/ Edible glue (see p. 23)
/ Needle nose pliers
/ Cornflour dusting pouch (see p. 43)
/ Firm foam pad with holes
  (aka 'Mexican Hat' foam pad)
/ Ball tool
/ Small non-stick rolling pin
/ Small paintbrush for glue
/ Knife modelling tool
/ Veining tool
/ Five-pointed jasmine or stephanotis
  blossom cutter
/ Florist's tape

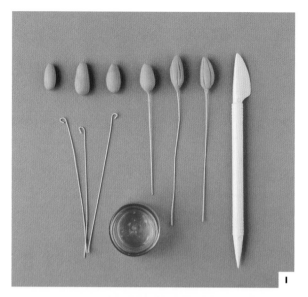

1

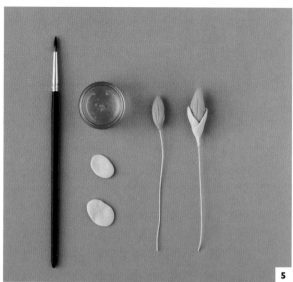

5

9

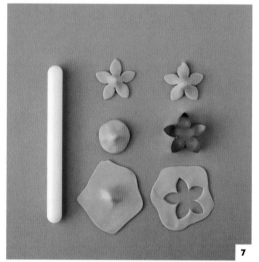

7

11

12

BUDS

1. Cut each length of florist's wire into four, each around 9cm long. Make a small hook at the end of each length using your pliers.

2. Take a small ball of pink flower paste and roll it into an elongated conical shape.

3. Dip the hooked end of a wire into the edible glue and push it through the base of the conical shape into the centre of the bud. Twist the end so it is firmly attached to the wire and pinch off any excess.

4. Using the knife modelling tool, make five indents from the top of the ball down the sides to form the centre bud. Leave to dry.

5. For the base of the bud, Take a small ball of green flower paste and squash it into an oval shape. Pinch one end between your fingers to thin out the edge. Repeat with another ball.

6. Dab some glue on the base of the bud. Take the thicker bottom edge of one of the ovals and wrap it around the base. Then dab some glue on the second and wrap it around the first. Leave to dry.

FLOWERS

7. Take a larger ball of pink flower paste and make a cone shape in the centre. Use a small rolling pin to roll out from the centre, making sure you leave the centre cone. You are aiming for a sombrero hat shape.

8. Place the blossom cutter centrally over the raised conical part and cut out, making sure you rub it firmly onto your workboard so there are no furry edges.

9. Flip the flower over and place the conical centre in a hole in the foam pad. Use the ball tool in an outward motion from the centre of each petal to the edge to thin the petals.

10. Use the knife tool to make an indent in the centre of each petal.

11. Take the hooked wire of step 1, and dip the hooked end into the edible glue. Then thread the unhooked end through the centre of the blossom. Pull the wire down through the blossom until the hooked end is hidden in the centre of the blossom. Twist the end of the cone onto the wire and make sure it's attached firmly, taking off any excess.

12. Make a centre for the blossom by gluing a tiny ball of pale green flower paste onto the centre.

MIXED STEM

13. To make a stem with buds and blossoms, take a short length of the florist's tape and stretch it to release the glue. Starting at the base of one bud, wrap the tape tightly around the wire. Then take the next bud and wrap the tape around them both. Continue in this way for another one or two buds, then start adding the blossoms.

Wired Roses

It's best to tackle roses as if you are an assembly line, making all the centres first, then the inner petals a few hours later, and so on. You need each stage to dry fully before adding the next layer of petals.

Equipment needed

/ No. 22 florist's wire

/ Cream flower paste

/ Pink flower paste

/ Edible glue (see p. 23)

/ Hot glue gun

/ Cornflour dusting pouch (see p. 43)

/ Firm foam pad

/ Ball tool

/ 20mm polystyrene ball

/ 65mm five-petal rose cutter

/ 75mm five-petal rose cutter

/ 80mm single petal cutter

/ Calyx cutter

/ Small non-stick rolling pin

/ Small paintbrush for glue

/ Soft paintbrush for dusting

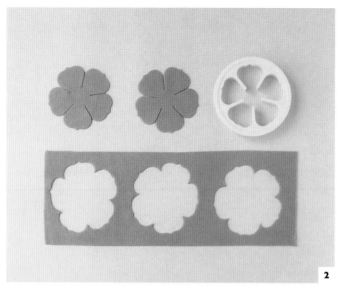

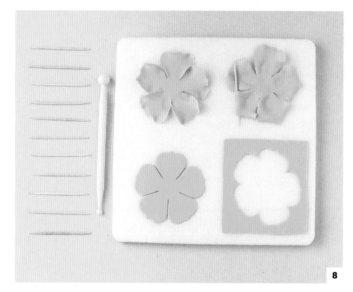

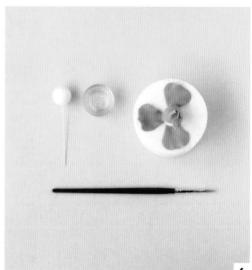

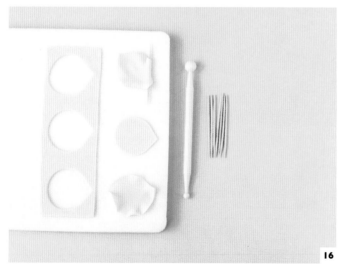

ROSEBUD CENTRE

1. Cut a length of no. 22 florist's wire into three equal parts, and with the hot glue gun, glue one length into the polystyrene ball.

2. Thinly roll out the pink flower paste and cut a shape using the 65mm five-petal rose cutter.

3. Place this shape onto your firm foam pad, and place the ball tool half on the paste and half on the foam pad. Then gently rub the ball tool along the edge of the petal to thin and give some movement to the petals. Flip the shape over and press the ball tool from the top edge of each petal towards the centre to cup each petal.

4. Place the flower-shape on the fingers of your left hand (if you're right-handed). Then take the ball on the wire from step 1 and thread the wire through the centre of the flower, between your fingers.

5. Imagine the petals are numbered clockwise: 1, 2, 3, 4 and 5. Brush petal 1 very lightly with edible glue. Then repeat with petal 3.

6. Wrap petal 1 around the polystyrene ball, leaving one side free. Now slot petal 3 into this gap, and wrap all the way around, so that the top of the polystyrene ball is fully covered.

7. Paint the remaining three petals (2, 4 and 5) just halfway up with glue, and bring them up so they loosely cover the first two, creating a rosebud shape. Leave to dry.

MIDDLE LAYER PETALS

8. Add some cream flower paste to the remaining pink and knead until you have a colour one shade lighter than that of the bud (you will do this with each layer of petals, so that there is a gentle gradation of colour from the centre to the edge of the rose). Roll the flower paste out and cut it using the 65mm five-petal rose cutter.

9. Thin the edges and cup the petals as per step 3. Use a cocktail stick to curl back the edges of each petal. Leave to dry until the shape is leather hard (about half an hour).

10. Paint glue on the outside edges of each petal, about halfway up from the centre.

11. Thread the bud through the centre, and attach the petals in an overlapping fashion.

12. Add some more cream flower paste to the remaining pink and knead well. Roll this out and cut out another layer of petals using the 75mm five-petal rose cutter.

13. Thin the edges and cup the petals as before. Use a cocktail stick to curl back the edges of each petal. Leave the shape to dry until it's leather hard.

14. Paint glue on the outside edges of each petal, about halfway up from the centre, and again, thread the wire through the centre, attaching the petals in an overlapping fashion.

15. Hang the rose upside down to dry fully (to make an impromptu flower drying rack, see p. 71).

EXTERNAL PETALS

16. Add some more cream flower paste to the remaining pink and knead well. Roll out thinly, and cut seven single petals using the 80mm petal cutter. Thin the edges and cup the petals, using a cocktail stick to curl back the edges of each petal. Leave to dry until they're leather hard.

17. Glue only the outside edges of each petal about halfway up from the centre.

18. Holding the rose upside down, glue the petals on in an overlapping fashion and leave to dry fully whilst hanging upside down.

19. Cut a calyx shape from the green flower paste. Thin the edges with the ball tool, thread through the wire and glue to the base of the rose.

JAZZ AGE

For this cake, I took the gorgeous Claire Pettibone dress worn by the bride as inspiration. I used a pearlised background to create contrast, allowing the embossed lace effect detailing to stand out.
The hanging lace 'beads' evoke 1920s flapper dresses.

This cake uses polystyrene cake separators between the tiers. This adds height and also provides space for the beads to hang freely.

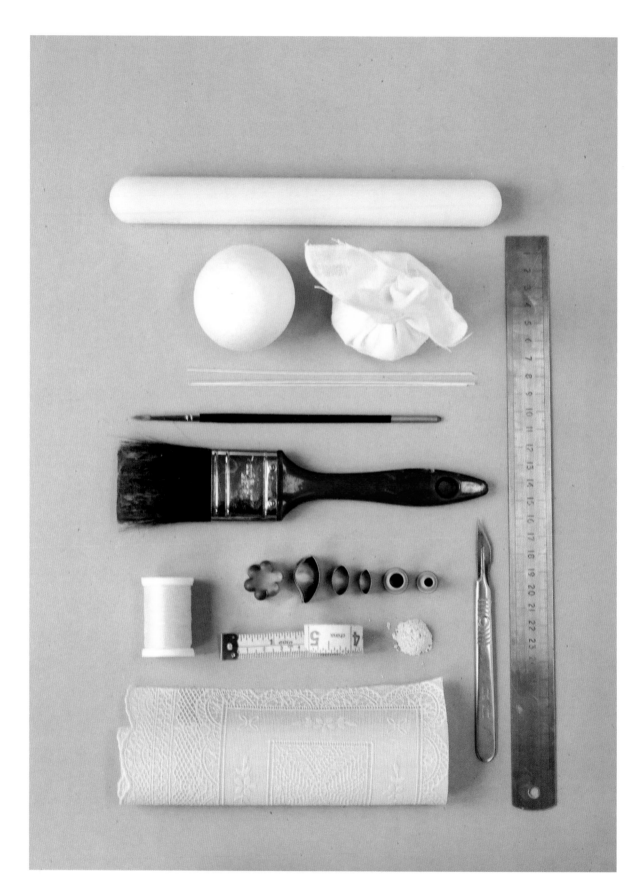

How To Make It

Techniques used
/ Embossing a lace texture
/ Dusting a tier with lustre dust
/ Making hanging 'beads'

Equipment needed
/ No. 20 florist's wire
/ Hot glue gun
/ 60mm polystyrene ball
/ 25mm leaf cutter
/ 25mm blossom cutter
/ 15mm oval cutter
/ 10mm oval cutter
/ 5mm round cutter
/ 8mm round cutter
/ Large soft brush
/ Pizza cutting wheel
/ Cream flower paste
/ Edible glue (see p. 23)
/ Ivory sugarpaste
/ Pearl lustre dust
/ Cornflour dusting pouch (see p. 43)
/ Steel ruler
/ Tape measure
/ Small non-stick rolling pin
/ Cotton thread
/ Small paintbrush
/ Plastic raised-pattern lace tablecloth
  or fabric
/ Baking paper

FOR YOUR BASE STRUCTURE

Start with
• 1 x 25cm x 10cm cake
• 1 x 22.5cm x 5cm polystyrene cake separator
• 1 x 20cm x 10cm cake
• 1 x 17.5cm x 5cm polystyrene cake separator
• 1 x 15cm x 15cm cake
• 1 x 10cm x 5cm cake or polystyrene cake separator
• 1 x 30cm cake drum

1. Glue cake cards to the base of the polystyrene separators, making sure the cards are the same width as their separators.

2. Cover all the cakes and separators with ivory sugarpaste and leave overnight to dry.

CREATING THE LUSTRED EFFECT

3. Rub the smallest amount of white vegetable fat over each tier. Buff with a soft paper kitchen towel to smooth out and remove any excess. Then use a large, soft brush (such as a 6cm-wide painter's brush) to brush the lustre dust over each tier.

4. Dowel and stack your cakes and the polystyrene separators.

CHEVRONS

Base tier chevrons

5. Cut a strip of baking paper so it measures 10cm x 84cm. Fold this in half widthways, then in half again, and then three more times, so you end up with a long, slim rectangle with 16 folds.

6. Mark 7cm up one side of the rectangle and cut diagonally from just above the base to this mark through all the layers.

7. Open it up and you have a strip of paper with zigzags cut out of the bottom. Wrap this around the base of the cake tier overlapping the ends, and secure with tape. This will be your guide for sticking on the chevron flower paste pattern.

8. Clean and dry the plastic raised-pattern lace tablecloth, then dust it gently with cornflour. Roll out some cream flower paste on top of the tablecloth to emboss the pattern into the paste.

9. Following the template on p. 190, use the steel ruler and scalpel to cut out 16 strips 8mm x 80mm of embossed flower paste. Trim the strips at a 45 degree angle at either end. Make sure you have eight strips facing one way and eight facing the other.

10. Paint edible glue on the back of these strips and attach to the cake in a chevron pattern, using your paper pattern as a guide.

Second tier chevrons

11. Cut a strip of baking paper 10cm x 70cm, fold as per step 5, then mark 5cm up one side and cut diagonally from just above the base to this mark.

12. Repeat steps 7-10, making the strips 8mm x 70mm.

Third tier chevrons

13. Cut a strip of baking paper 15cm x 54cm. Fold as per step 5, then mark 3cm up one side and cut diagonally from just above the base to this mark.

14. Repeat steps 7-10, making the strips 8mm x 45mm.

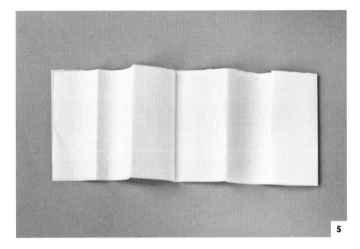

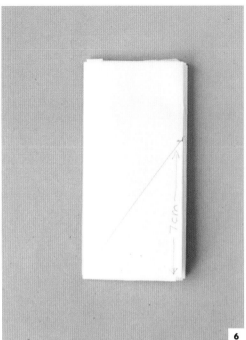

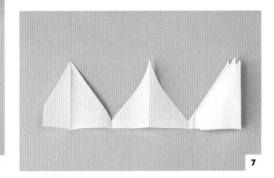

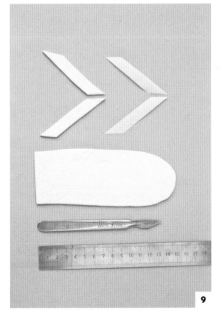

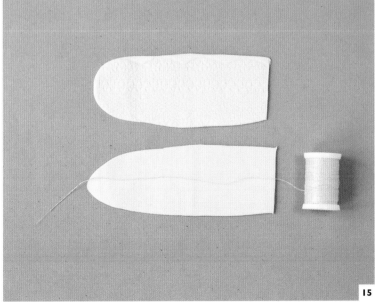

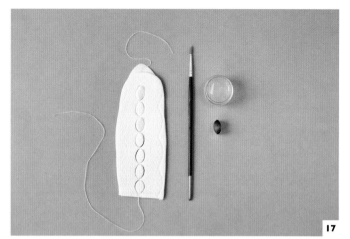

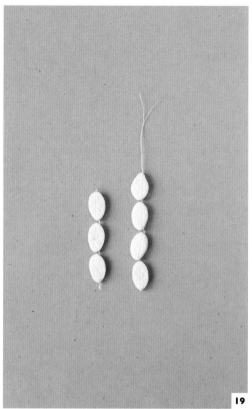

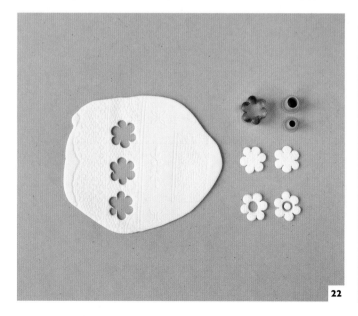

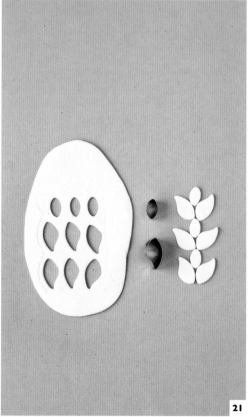

HANGING BEADS

15. Take some more cream flower paste and roll it out on the tablecloth to emboss the pattern. Cut two strips of 4cm x 12cm.

16. Place one strip pattern-side down, and lay a strip of cotton thread lengthwise down its centre. Brush over it with edible glue, then place the second strip on top, pattern side up.

17. Use the 15mm oval cutter to cut a string of seven ovals. The ovals will stay connected to one another with the cotton thread, like beads. Make 16 strings of seven ovals.

18. Paint a bit of glue on the top three beads of these strings and attach them to the cake under the apex of each chevron on the base and second tier.

19. Using the same method as in step 16, make 32 strings of four beads each, and 26 strings of three beads each. Glue the four-bead strings on either side of the seven-bead strings. Glue the three-bead strings at the base of each chevron.

LEAF PATTERN

20. Roll out some more cream flower paste on top of the tablecloth to emboss the pattern into the paste. Cut out 56 leaf shapes and 28 of the 15mm oval shapes.

21. Glue the leaves on in the pattern shown in the 'V' of the chevrons. Alternate columns of three-leaf patterns and four-leaf patterns.

FLOWER PATTERN

22. Roll out some more cream flower paste on top of the tablecloth to emboss the pattern into the paste. Cut out 28 of the 10mm ovals and eight blossoms. Cut holes in centres of the blossoms using the 8mm round cutter.

23. Measure and mark with a scriber eight regular intervals around the base of the this tier and glue the blossoms at these points. Glue a pair of ovals in a 'V' shape in between each blossom. Then glue the remaining ovals just above these in alternating vertical columns of three ovals and four ovals, as per the main image on p. 110.

24. Cut out tiny circles using the 5mm round cutter, and attach to the centre of the blossoms.

LACE BALL ORNAMENT

25. Take a 60mm polystyrene ball and hot glue a 10cm length of no. 20 florist's wire to it.

26. Paint edible glue lightly all over the ball and cover it with sugarpaste. Leave to dry, then brush on lustre dust.

27. Roll out cream flower paste on top of the tablecloth to emboss the pattern into the paste, and cut out 30 blossom shapes. Cut holes in the blossoms using the 8mm round cutter. Glue the blossoms to the ball.

28. Cut out tiny circles using the 5mm round cutter and attach to the centre of the blossoms.

29. Push a posy pick (see p. 54) containing a small amount of modelling paste into the centre of the top tier and insert the wire into this.

ORCHIDS
AND
ANEMONES

Sometimes no colour is needed.
An ivory cake with ivory icing creates
a simple but striking design, allowing you
to focus on the shadows and shapes of the
cake and the flowers. It reminds me a bit
of the marble statues from Ancient Greece
in the British Museum that I used to draw
back in my art college days.

Anemones are striking flowers, often found
in deep pinks, reds, and purples. I have
used them in a stylised version here along
with the extravagantly frilly
cattelya orchid.

How To Make It

Techniques used

/ Making and using moulds

/ Making cattelya orchids

/ Making anemones

/ Making cutter flowers

Equipment needed for the cake

/ Royal icing

/ No. 2 piping tip

/ Paper piping bag (see p. 25)

FOR YOUR BASE STRUCTURE

Start with:

- 1 x 25cm x 10cm cake
- 1 x 20cm x 20cm cake
- 1 x 17.5cm x 5cm cake (this layer could be a polystyrene dummy)
- 1 x 15cm x 10cm cake
- 1 x 7.5cm x 5cm cake (this layer could be a polystyrene dummy)
- 1 x 30cm cake drum

1. Cover all the tiers and cake drum with ivory sugarpaste. Leave overnight to dry.

2. Dowel and stack your cakes.

3. Attach a 15mm ivory grosgrain ribbon to the base of each tier and around the drum.

FLOWERS

4. Following the instructions on the pages indicated make the following flowers:
   - Six ivory cattelya orchids (p. 128)
   - Six large, ivory stylised anemones (p. 132)
   - Ten ivory hydrangeas (p. 98)
   - Ten ivory eight-petalled cutter flowers with moulded centres (p. 90)

TOP TIER BOUQUET

5. Using white florist's tape, tape three orchid flowers together so they are lined up vertically, one above the other. Stretch the florist's tape before using to release the glue.

6. Insert a posy pick (see p. 54) in the centre of the top tier. Cut all the wires to the correct length, and insert the orchids into the posy pick. If the flowers move, you can either pipe some royal icing into the posy pick, or put in some sugarpaste to hold the orchid arrangement in place. If you are transporting the cake, it may be safer to insert the bouquet once the cake has been set up on the table.

ATTACHING THE FLOWERS

7. In order to create a cascading effect for the flowers, insert a posy pick onto the ledge between the base tier and second tier. Insert one cattelya orchid with a short wire into this, and a second with a longer wire. To prevent movement, attach one petal of the taller orchid to the cake with a dot of royal icing.

8. On the ledge of the fourth tier, insert a single orchid into a posy pick.

9. Attach the anemones, hydrangea and blossom flowers by piping a dot of royal icing on the cake and then holding the flower on it for ten seconds or so. It's best to start with the larger anemones, and then fill in the gaps with the smaller hydrangeas and blossoms. To achieve the best effect, position more larger flowers at the bottom, with the smaller flowers less densely spaced as you go further up the cake.

Cattleya Orchid

Equipment needed

- / No. 18 florist's wire
- / No. 26 florist's wire
- / Florist's tape
- / Ivory flower paste
- / Edible glue (see p. 23)
- / Firm foam pad
- / Cardboard tube centre from a roll of paper towel
- / Ball tool
- / Knife tool
- / Cattelya orchid cutters
- / Leaf veining board
- / Wire cutters
- / Small non-stick rolling pin
- / Small paintbrush for glue
- / Veining tool

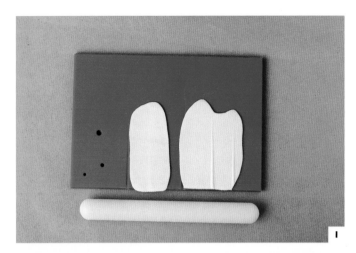

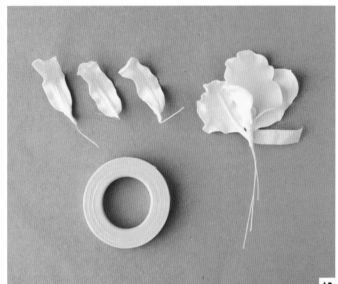

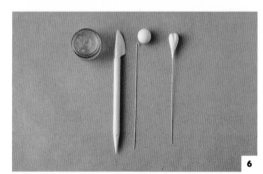

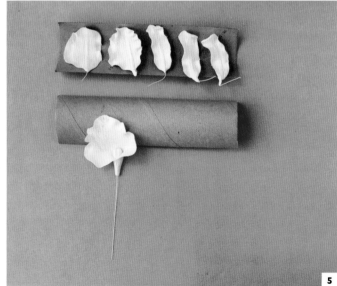

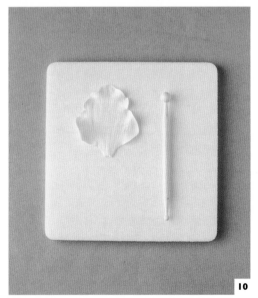

EXTERNAL PETALS

1. Roll the ivory flower paste thinly over one of the indentations on the leaf veining board. This will create a thicker central part, into which you will be threading wire.

2. Cut three of the thinner sepal shapes and two petal shapes out of the flower paste, keeping the thicker part central to the shapes.

3. Cut the no. 26 wire into three equal lengths. Paint edible glue about 2cm up the wire, and very carefully thread this through the thick central part of each petal. Twist the very end of the petal to secure it to the wire.

4. Roll the veiner tool on the petal to impress the veins, being careful not to go over the thicker central part that has the wire inserted. Then place the flower parts on the firm foam pad and use the ball tool to thin out the edges.

5. Cut your cardboard tube in half lengthwise. Place your petals on the inside curve of the tube and leave to dry.

CENTRAL PETAL AND COLUMN

6. The column is the teardrop-shaped centre of the orchid, which carries the reproductive organs of the flower. To make the column, hook the end of one wire and dip it in the edible glue. Push this through a small ball of flower paste and pinch the bottom to secure the wire, making a teardrop shape. Use the knife tool to make an indentation across the top. Set aside to dry.

7. Roll out the ivory flower paste thinly over one of the indentations on the leaf veining board, as per step 1.

8. Cut the large central petal shape. Paint the bottom 2cm of your florist's wire with edible glue, and very carefully thread this through the thick central part of the petal. Twist the very end of the petal to secure it to the wire.

9. Roll the veiner tool on the petal to add some veins, being careful not to roll over the thicker central part that has the wire inserted.

10. Place on the firm foam pad and use the ball tool to thin out the edges, this time pressing quite hard to achieve a frilled edge.

11. Brush a small amount of edible glue on the very base and sides of the petal, then place the column on this, and wrap the base of the petal around it. Take the second half of your cardboard tube, and leave the parts to dry on the outer curve of the tube.

ASSEMBLING THE ORCHID

12. Hold the wired central petal with the column upside down and tape the two external petals to the main wire, making sure they sit on either side of the central petal.

13. Attach the three sepals with the florist's tape. One sepal should be on top, in between the two side petals, and the other two sepals should sit below it.

Anemones

Equipment needed

/ Flower paste (these ones use dark pink and black, but for the Orchids and Anemones cake, you'll need to use ivory flower paste)

/ Edible glue (see p. 23)

/ Firm foam pad

/ Ball tool

/ Small non-stick rolling pin

/ Mould for centre

/ Small paintbrush for glue

/ Anemone cutter (this comes as a set with a large six-petal shape, a medium four-petal shape and a small two-petal shape.)

/ Cardboard apple tray

/ Veining tool

/ Black stamens or mould for centre

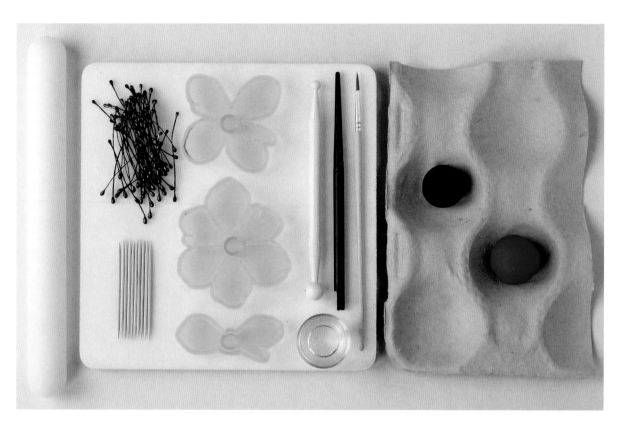

5

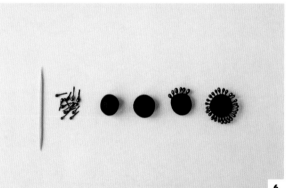

6

9

1. Roll out some flower paste thinly and cut out one large six-petal shape, one four-petal shape, and two of the small two-petal shapes.

2. Vein each petal with the veining tool, then place on the firm foam pad and thin the edges using the ball tool.

3. Place the first layer of petals (the six-petal shape) in the indent of the apple tray.

4. Paint a tiny bit of glue in the centre and place the second layer of petals (the four-petal shape) on top in such a way that the petals are staggered.

5. Paint a tiny bit of glue in the centre and place the third and fourth layer of petals (the two-petal shapes) on top, again so the petals are staggered.

CENTRE

6. Make a small ball of black flower paste and flatten slightly Make small pinpricks in this with a cocktail stick.

7. Take a handful of black stamens (around 20) and trim them so they measure 2cm long.

8. Dip the end of each stamen into edible glue then push into the black centre all the way around the edge and leave to dry.

9. Paint some glue onto the centre of the flower and glue the black centre and stamens on.

> ### TIP
> To make the ivory anemones seen in the Orchids and Anemones cake, skip steps 6-8, and instead make a centre mould from an ornate button (see p. 88 for making a mould).

ENCHANTED FOREST

This cake was created to reflect the outdoor forest setting of a very special wedding. You could easily replace the forest animal shapes I have used here with your own.

This cake requires some deft scalpel usage. Make sure you use a new sterile blade for each project — they're easy to pick up at art and hobby shops.

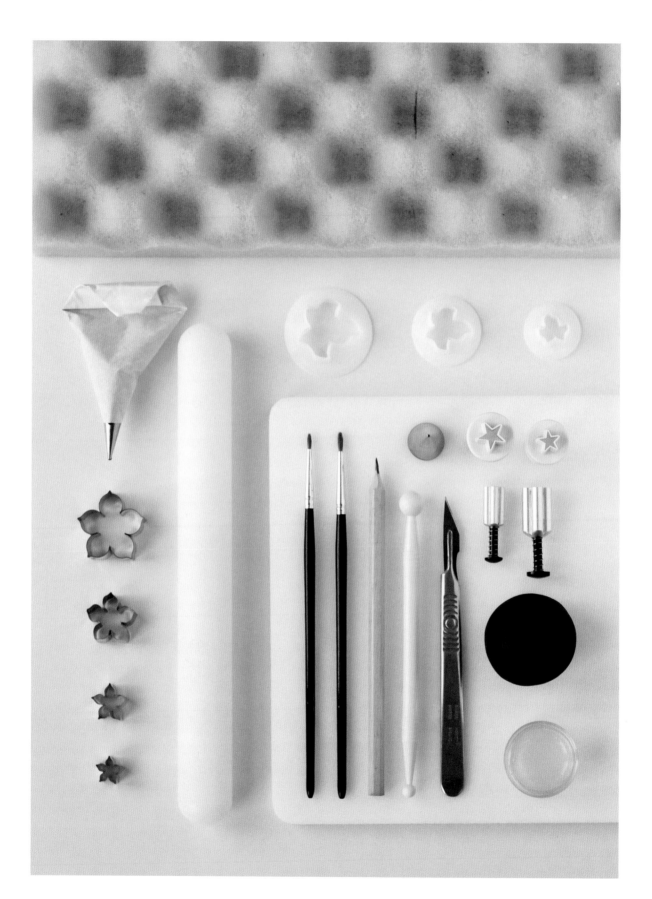

How To Make It

Techniques used

/ Cutter flowers
/ Piping royal icing
/ Cutting out and attaching shapes

Equipment needed

/ Set of three ivy leaf cutters: 25mm,
  20mm and 12mm
/ Petunia cutters in the following sizes:
  10mm, 15mm and 22mm
/ 15mm and 10mm blossom cutters
/ 15mm and 10mm star cutters
/ Scalpel
/ Baking paper or tracing paper
/ Sharp pencil
/ Ball tool
/ Firm foam pad
/ Dimple foam
/ Small paintbrush
/ Black flower paste
/ Edible glue (see p. 23)
/ Royal icing coloured black (see p. 24)
/ No. 1.5 piping tip
/ Paper piping bag (see p. 24)

FOR YOUR BASE STRUCTURE

Start with
- 1 x 35cm x 10cm cake
- 1 x 25cm x 10cm cake
- 1 x 20cm x 20cm cake
- 1 x 10cm x 10cm cake
- 1 x 40cm cake drum

1. Cover all the tiers and the cake drum with ivory sugarpaste. Leave overnight to dry. The next day, dowel and stack your cakes.

2. Attach a 15mm ivory grosgrain ribbon to the base of each tier and around the drum.

ANIMALS AND GRASSES

3. Thinly roll out the black flower paste and leave to dry for around ten minutes until it's leather hard.

4. Using baking paper or tracing paper, trace three of each deer, two hares and the grasses from the templates on p. 190.

5. Place your tracing paper on the flower paste and trace over the shapes again using a very sharp pencil. You should be left with an indented outline on the flower paste, which you can now carefully cut with a scalpel. Place the cut out shapes inside a plastic folder so they don't dry out before you're ready to attach them.

6. The problem with black flower paste is that it might leave a mark on the white cake if you move it around when you're attaching it. To make it a little easier to get the placement of the shapes right, smear a tiny bit of vegetable fat on a piece of acetate, and using a small palette knife, place the shapes on the acetate.

7. Brush some edible glue on one of the shapes and then hold the acetate on the base tier, just above the ribbon, finding the right position for the shape. When you are happy with the placement, gently rub the back of the acetate to transfer the shape to the cake.

BASE TIER FLOWERS

8. Thinly roll out some more black flower paste and cut out a selection of the flowers and stars from the 15mm and 10mm petunia cutters, the 15mm and 10mm blossom cutters and the 15mm and 10mm star cutters (around 100 flowers in total). Place the larger pieces in the dimple foam, and the tiny ones on the firm foam. Gently cup and thin the flowers using the ball tool.

9. Pipe a small dot of black royal icing onto the back of each flower, and attach it to the cake by holding it in place for a few seconds.

10. Pipe small pearls of icing in the flower centres. Pipe some small groups of tiny dots to fill in the spaces.

SECOND TIER DECORATIONS

11. Thinly roll out some more black flower paste and cut a selection of flowers using the 15mm and 10mm petunia cutters and the 15mm and 10mm star cutters (around 200 flowers). Place the larger pieces in the dimple foam and the tiny ones on the firm foam. Gently cup and thin them using the ball tool.

12. Pipe a small dot of black royal icing onto the back of the flower, and hold in place on the cake for a few seconds to attach.

13. Pipe small pearls of icing in the centres of each flower. Pipe some swirly lines and dots in between the flowers to fill in the gaps.

THIRD TIER DECORATIONS

14. Pipe some swirly, looping lines draping down from the top of this tier to represent twisted vines. Pipe some that reach down nearly to the base and some shorter ones.

15. Thinly roll out some more black flower paste, and cut out a selection of all the ivy leaves (about 50 of each size). Place on the firm foam pad. Gently cup and thin the leaves using the ball tool.

16. Pipe a small dot of black royal icing onto the back of each leaf and attach it to the cake by holding it in place for a few seconds. Start with the larger leaves, and then attach the smaller ones.

TOP TIER DECORATIONS

17. Thinly roll out some more black flower paste and cut out a selection of all the petunia flowers (about 30 of each size). Place the larger pieces in the dimple foam, and the smaller ones on the firm foam. Gently cup and thin the flowers using the ball tool.

18. Pipe a small dot of black royal icing onto the back of each flower, and attach it to the cake by holding it in place for a few seconds. Attach the larger flowers at the top first, then the medium and smaller sized ones below, spacing them out more as you come down the cake.

5

8

10

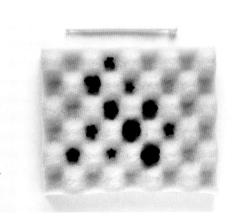

8

11

14

SLEEPING BEAUTY

"And, in that very moment,
she fell down upon the bed that stood there,
and lay in a deep sleep. And this sleep
extended over the whole palace..."
– Sleeping Beauty, The Brothers Grimm

This cake was inspired by the romantic
fairytale, Sleeping Beauty. The story goes
that a princess was put to sleep by an evil
fairy for 100 years. The prince broke the
enchantment by fighting his way through
the thorny rosebushes that had grown to
surround the castle, to reach the princess
and wake her with a kiss.

How To Make It

Techniques used
- / Painting with metallic edible paint
- / Making fantasy roses with jewelled centres
- / Making wired leaves

Equipment needed
- / Small flat-ended paintbrush
- / Royal icing coloured pale yellow/brown
- / No. 2 piping tip
- / Paper piping bag (see p. 24)
- / Gold edible paint
- / Stainless steel ruler
- / Scriber or toothpick

FOR YOUR BASE STRUCTURE:

Start with
- 1 x 30cm x 10cm cake
- 1 x 20cm x 10cm cake
- 1 x 15cm x 10cm cake
- 1 x 10cm x 10cm cake
- 1 x 36cm cake drum

1. Colour the sugarpaste a pale pink. Do this a day in advance as the paste requires a lot of kneading, and it will be too warm and soft to use straight away. Wrap in a plastic bag and leave to rest overnight – this will also allow time for the colour to develop.

2. Cover the tiers and the cake drum in pale pink sugar paste. Leave overnight to dry. Don't dowel and stack your cakes yet.

PAINTING GOLD LINES

3. Start by marking guidelines for the paint on the base tier. To mark an even line, hold a steel ruler vertically against the side of the tier, and place a toothpick at 1.5cm from the base in such a way that the point of the toothpick is just touching the cake. Holding the ruler and toothpick together, carefully slide them around the cake, so that you scribe a light horizontal line 1.5cm from the bottom.

4. Repeat, making two more guidelines at 4.5cm and 5.5cm up from the base, and then again, making two further guidelines at 8cm and 9cm up from the base.

5. Take your edible gold paint (you can either use readymade paint or mix a small amount of vodka with gold dust), and paint between these guidelines with the flat-ended brush, making a 1.5cm-wide line at the base, and two 1cm-wide lines further up.

6. Now move onto the second (20cm) tier. Mark a horizontal guideline at 3.5cm from the base, and then again at 8cm and 9cm up from the base. Paint in with gold paint as before.

7. For the third (15cm) tier, mark a horizontal guideline as before at 2.5cm up from the base. Paint in as before.

8. For the fourth (10cm) tier, mark guidelines at 3cm up from the base and then again at 4cm and 5cm up from the base. Mark one more set of guidelines at 7cm and 8cm up from the base. Paint in between the guidelines as before.

9. Attach the base tier to the cake drum using royal icing and then dowel and stack all the tiers.

MAKING THE ROSES AND LEAVES

10. Following the instructions on p. 152, make the following:
    - Four small roses using 40mm polystyrene balls, each rose to have one first layer of 42mm petals and a second layer of 60mm petals.
    - Three medium roses using 40mm polystyrene balls, each rose to have one first layer of 42mm petals, and a second and third layer of 60mm petals.
    - Three large roses using 50mm polystyrene balls, each rose to have one layer of 60mm petals, a second layer of 80mm petals and the third layer with seven 80mm petals.
    - One extra large rose using a 50mm polystyrene ball with one layer of 60mm petals, and second, third and fourth layers of seven 80mm petals.
    - Nine large leaves and 12 small leaves.

ATTACHING THE ROSES

11. Some of the roses will be secured to the cake with royal icing, and others will have wires inserted into posy picks. Before you start, hold the roses up to the cake and try to find a pleasing arrangement. Start from the base tier and work your way up the cake.

12. For the top tier, take three large roses and trim their wires so that they are flush to the base (ie. invisible). Pipe a large dot of stiff royal icing on the top, and hold one of the roses on this for two or three minutes, until the icing sets enough to secure it. If it's still loose, pipe more royal icing to keep in place. Repeat for the other two roses.

13. Insert a posy pick (see p. 54) centrally on the top ledge of the base tier, with a small cone of sugar paste inside it. Trim the wire of the extra large rose to length, and insert it into the posy pick. You may need to pipe a dot of royal icing where the rose touches the cake to keep it in place.

14. Insert another posy pick with a small cone of sugar paste inside it just to one side of the first rose. Trim the wire of a medium rose to length and insert into this posy pick.

15. Repeat on the top ledge of the second (20cm) tier, this time using one medium and one small rose.

16. Trim the wire of a small rose flush with the base of the rose. Pipe a dot of stiff royal icing on the side of the cake just above the two roses you have just attached. Hold the small rose on the icing for a few minutes to attach. This rose should rest on the two roses below, which will help to support it, you may also want to pipe some royal icing on these two roses where the small rose touches them for extra security.

17. Repeat steps 13 and 14 using one medium and one small rose on top of the third (15cm) tier.

18. Hold the leaves to gauge where they work best with the roses. Cut the wires to length and either insert into the posy picks, or use royal icing to attach the leaves to the side of the cake.

Fantasy Roses

These extravagant open roses have jewelled centres and a plethora of leaves. Here painted in gold for added opulence, but of course could be coloured to suit your scheme.

Equipment needed

/ No. 24 gold florist's wire
/ No. 20 florist's wire
/ Gold stamens (approx 20 per rose)
/ Flower paste coloured pale beige
/ Gold lustre dust
/ Edible gold paint
/ Edible glue (see p. 23)
/ Hot glue gun
/ Cornflour dusting pouch (see p. 43)
/ Firm foam pad
/ Ball tool
/ 40mm polystyrene ball
/ 50mm round cutter
/ Rose petal cutters in the following sizes: 42mm, 60mm and 80mm
/ Rose leaf cutters in 80mm and 90mm
/ 60mm calyx cutter
/ Small non-stick rolling pin
/ Small paintbrush for glue
/ Small flat-ended paintbrush for dusting

1

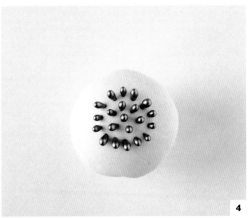

4

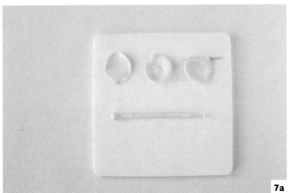

7a

5

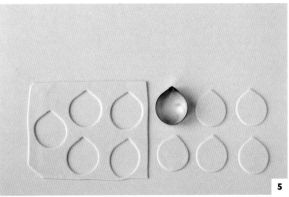

12

16

14

JEWELLED CENTRES

1. Cut each no. 20 wire into three lengths of about 12cm long. Use the hot glue gun to glue the ends of the wires into a 40mm polystyrene ball.

2. Roll out some of the pale beige flower paste to about 2mm thick and cut out a circle using the 5cm round cutter. Brush one side with edible glue and stick on the top of the polystyrene ball.

3. Cut off the ends of the stamens so there is just the gold 'bead' and a very small part of the wire left.

4. Stick these stamens into the circle of flower paste on the polystyrene ball. Start with one in the centre, then radiate outwards. You should use about 20 stamens.

PETALS

5. Roll out more flower paste quite thinly. Cut out five petals with the 42mm petal cutter.

6. Place one petal onto your firm foam pad and place the ball tool half on the paste and half on the foam pad. Then gently rub the ball tool along the edge of the petal to thin and give it some movement.

7. Flip the petal over and press the ball tool from the top edge of towards the centre to cup the petal. Then roll the top edge of the petal over a toothpick. Place in an apple tray until leather hard.

8. Repeat for the other four petals and paint edible glue on the bottom third of each petal.

9. Hold the jewelled centre upside down and glue one petal to the base of the ball. Make sure the rolled top edge of the petal is slightly higher than the stamens.

10. Glue the other four petals on, overlapping each one. Leave to dry upside down (to make an impromptu flower drying stand, see p. 71).

11. Once dry, cut five more petals using the 60mm petal cutter and repeat steps 8-12.

FINISHING

12. Cut out a calyx for the rose from the beige flower paste. Paint edible glue on one side of the calyx and then thread through the wire and glue on the base of the rose. This will cover up any of the polystyrene ball still showing. Leave to dry.

13. Using the flat-edged brush, dust the flowers with the gold lustre dust, dusting more gold on the very edges of the petals.

LEAVES

14. Roll out some beige flower paste to about 1mm thickness and cut out a leaf shape. Rub a small rolling pin over the back of the cutter to get rid of any furry edges. You may need to ease the leaves out of the cutter using a toothpick.

15. Paint a 3cm line of edible glue in the centre of each leaf, starting from the bottom edge of the leaf. Cut each gold wire in half, and place a wire on the leaf where it has been glued.

16. Fold the leaf over at the base, enclosing the wire. Pinch this together and pinch the paste at the very base of the leaf to make sure it's secured firmly to the wire.

17. Open the leaf out and thin the edges of the leaf using the ball tool on the firm foam pad. Leave to dry fully in the apple tray.

18. Make a gold paint by either mixing a little vodka with the lustre dust, or use a readymade edible gold paint to paint the backs of the leaf. Leave this to dry fully before painting the front.

ART DECO

Art Deco has been a popular wedding theme for the past few years. This cake design references the geometric style of that period, and softens it with pearl buttons and delicate, but quite stylised painted roses, inspired by textiles and fashions of the 1920s and '30s.

The decorative mouldings on this cake are easily done using an extruder gun. The hand-painting is also easier than you might think. The large roses on the top have delicate black-edged petals, which echo the painted roses around the edges.

How To Make It

Techniques used

/ Using an extruder gun

/ Painting directly onto the cake

/ Making roses

/ Using an edible marker

/ Making pearl buttons

Equipment needed

/ Sugarcraft extruder gun

/ White vegetable fat

/ Peach coloured modelling paste
  (see p. 20)

/ Peach coloured flower paste

/ Black flower paste

/ Cornflour dusting pouch (see p. 43)

/ Pearl metallic paint

/ Craft knife

/ Scriber tool

/ Steel ruler

/ Edible glue (see p. 23)

/ Black paste food colour

/ Peach paste food colour

/ Black edible marker pen

/ White edible dust colour

/ Baking parchment paper

/ Artist's palette

/ Vodka

/ Small paintbrush

FOR YOUR BASE STRUCTURE

Start with

- 1 x 30cm x 10cm cake
- 1 x 20cm x 20cm cake
- 1 x 25cm x 5cm cake (this tier could be a polystyrene cake dummy instead of cake)
- 1 x 15cm x 5cm cake (this tier could be a polystyrene cake dummy instead of cake)
- 1 x 40cm cake drum

1. Cover the tiers and the cake drum in ivory sugarpaste and leave overnight to dry. Don't dowel and stack your cakes yet.

PAINTED ROSES

Base tier and top tier

2. Make your paint: Mix a small amount of the peach paste food colour with a tiny amount of the white edible dust and enough vodka to create a paintable consistency. The vodka is tasteless and evaporates once dry, and doesn't dissolve the sugarpaste. The white edible dust makes the colour opaque. Mix the proportions to get the right shade – to make it paler either add more vodka or more white dust.

3. Paint roundish shapes in the peach colour at the top edge of the base tier. These should vary in size from 1.5cm to 4cm. Leave to dry.

4. Paint the details of the roses. You can either use a black edible marker, or you can make paint by mixing black paste food colour with vodka and use a fine paintbrush to apply. Start from the centre and work the petals outwards, using the template on p. 191 as a guide. You might want to practice on paper first.

5. Now do the same for the top tier, this time covering the tier with roses.

Third tier painted roses

6. Cut a strip of baking paper to 68cm x 10cm. Fold it in half widthwise, then fold in half widthwise twice more. Your paper should now be 8.5cm x 10cm.

7. Cut the shape following the template "A" on p. 191. Open out and wrap around the base of the third tier, securing with sellotape.

8. Use the scriber tool or a toothpick to mark along the edge of the template. Then remove the paper template and paint roses as per steps 3 and 4 from these marked points down to the base of the tier.

EXTRUDED MOULDINGS

9. Trace and cut out two of the template labelled "B" on p. 191. Place each of these on the third tier with the "arrow tip" pointing downwards and 2cm above the point which is labelled "b1" on the template "A" used in step 7. Scribe around as before.

10. Trace and cut out two paper templates of the template labelled "C" on p. 191. Place each of these with the point 2cms above the point which is labelled "b1" on the template "A" used in step 7. Scribe around as before.

11. Knead some white vegetable fat into the peach sugarpaste to soften it up. Insert the disc with the raised centre into the gun. Fill with the softened sugarpaste. Press the trigger repeatedly to extrude the sugarpaste as strips.

12. Glue the moulded strips onto the third tier along the scribed outlines of steps 8-10, trimming with a small sharp knife as necessary to create the corners and points.

13. Carefully paint the raised central ridge of the mouldings with the pearl metallic paint.

BUTTONS

14. Make 68 pea-sized balls of paste. Flatten them slightly by pressing with your finger. Leave to dry, then paint with the pearl metallic paint.

15. Glue eight buttons in the centres of the large upside down arrow shapes, and four in the smaller ones. Glue the rest of the buttons at the corners of the mouldings. These will hide any unsightly cuts.

ASSEMBLING THE TIERS

16. Dowel and stack your cakes.

17. Glue more extruded moulded strips at the bases of tiers 1 and 2. Carefully paint the raised central ridge of the mouldings with the pearl metallic paint.

TOP TIER ROSES

18. Following the instructions on p. 106, make three roses using peach flower paste in the following sizes:
    • One small rose using a 25mm polystyrene ball centre and two layers of petals (five petals in total). This rose should be a finished height of 5cm.
    • One medium rose using a 35mm polystyrene ball centre and three layers of petals (12 petals in total). This rose should be a finished height of 7cm.
    • One large rose using a 50mm polystyrene ball centre and three layers of petals (12 petals in total). This rose should be a finished height of 10cm. Leave to dry.

19. Using the black edible marker pen, mark the very edges of the petals. (you can also use a paintbrush and black edible paint, but it's trickier to get a neat line).

20. Roll out the black flower paste and cut a calyx for each rose, thinning out the edges on the firm foam pad with the ball tool.

21. Paint some edible glue on the centre of the calyx and about halfway up each section. Thread the centre of the calyx through the wire of the rose, rolling back the pointed tips of the calyx. Leave to dry.

22. Cut off the wires close to the calyx and attach the roses to the top tier with royal icing.

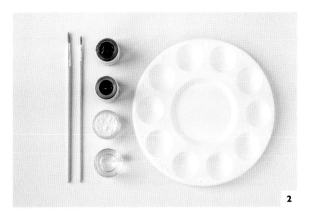

2

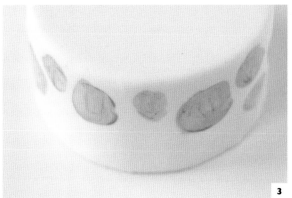

3

11

4

13

14

AUDREY HEPBURN

This cake was designed for a very chic city wedding. The brief was metallic, simple and contemporary, with Audrey Hepburn's classic style as inspiration. I responded by using a combination of silver leaf and a pearlised finish, with decorations of moth orchids. Black velvet ribbons around the base of the tiers create contrast and texture and add a certain '60s glamour.

How To Make It

Techniques used

/ Using silver leaf

/ Dusting with metallic edible lustre dusts

/ Making moth orchids and buds

/ Making miniature orchids

Equipment needed

/ Edible glue (see p. 23)

/ Edible pearl lustre dust

/ 4cm wide soft pastry or decorator's brush

/ Large, soft painting brush

/ Pearl lustre dust

/ 25 x 80mm x 80mm edible silver leaf
('transfer' silver leaf is attached to backing
paper, and is much easier to use than loose
sheets of silver leaf)

/ White vegetable fat

/ Paper towel

/ 1m lengths of black velvet ribbon in
the following widths: 38mm, 16mm
and 6mm

FOR YOUR BASE STRUCTURE

Start with

- 1 x 20cm x 15cm cake
- 1 x 15cm x 15cm cake
- 1 x 12.5cm x 5cm cake (this layer could be a
  polystyrene dummy)
- 1 x 30cm cake drum

1. Cover all the tiers and cake drum with white
   sugarpaste.

APPLYING SILVER LEAF

2. Lightly brush the base tier with cooled boiling water. Don't use a lot – just enough to make the sugarpaste tacky, not wet.

3. Starting at the bottom of the tier, take one square of silver leaf still on its backing paper and gently press against the cake. Buff over the backing sheet with a soft paper towel to smooth the leaf and make sure it adheres to the cake. Then carefully peel off the backing sheet.

4. Continue in this way, overlapping each new square of silver leaf very slightly. Work your way around the bottom tier and then move upwards. When you get to the top, fold the leaves over the top of the tier, covering the first 3cm (at least) of the top of the tier. Don't be tempted to try and rub off any loose bits of the silver leaf until it's completely dry. You can then use a soft brush to gently brush off any loose bits of silver leaf.

5. Repeat for the sides and top of the top tier.

APPLYING PEARL LUSTRE DUST

6. Very lightly smear the smallest amount of white vegetable fat all over the middle tier and the cake drum. Then buff this with a folded piece of soft paper towel to ensure only the lightest covering of fat is left on the cake.

7. Pour some pearl lustre dust onto a fresh paper towel. Dip your soft 4cm-wide brush in the dust and tap it on the paper towel to remove any excess. Brush the lustre dust on the cake tier, making sure your brushstrokes are all in the same direction.

8. Cover the tier completely with the dust and then repeat for the cake drum.

ASSEMBLING THE TIERS

9. Dowel and stack your cakes.

10. Attach the 38mm ribbon around the bottom tier. Attach the 6mm ribbon around the middle and top tiers. Attach the 16mm ribbon around the edge of the cake drum.

ORCHID STEMS

11. Make two stems of ivory moth orchids with six buds and three orchid flowers on each stem (see p. 172). Make one stem of orchids with four orchid flowers.

12. Make two stems of ivory miniature orchids with five orchids on each stem (see p. 176). Make one stem with four miniature orchids.

13. Insert a posy pick (see p. 54) into the top tier and arrange the orchids so the stems with buds are sticking up, and the longer stems and the miniature orchids drape over the edge.

Moth Orchid and Buds

Equipment needed

/ No. 24 florist's wire
/ No. 26 florist's wire
/ No. 20 florist's wire
/ Florist's tape
/ Ivory flower paste
/ Edible glue (see p. 23)
/ Small paintbrush
/ Firm foam pad
/ Cardboard apple trays
/ Ball tool
/ Knife tool
/ Craft knife
/ Moth orchid cutter and veiner set
/ Wire cutters
/ Small pliers
/ Small non-stick rolling pin
/ Small paintbrush for glue
/ Veining tool

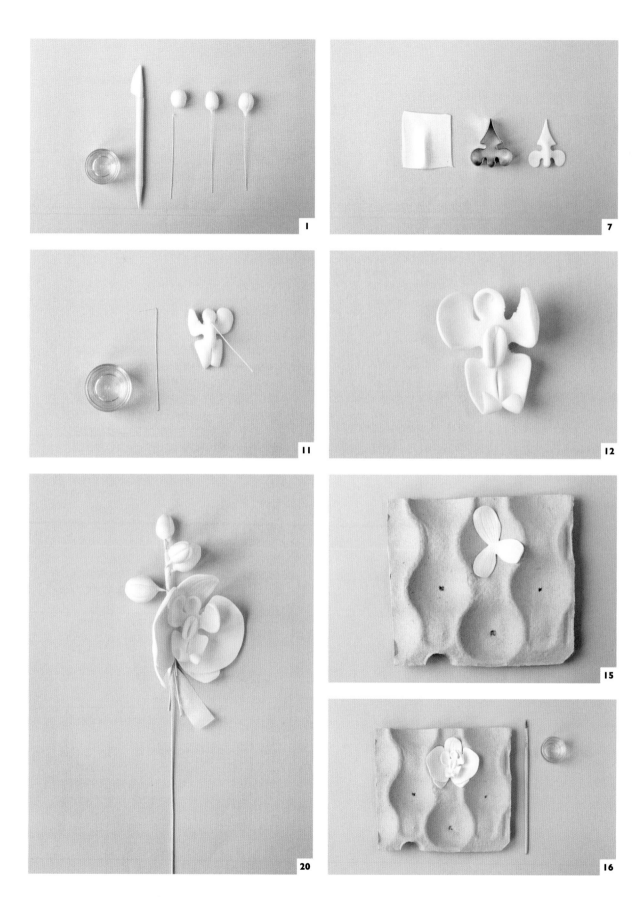

BUDS

1. Cut a piece of no. 24 florist's wire into three equal lengths, each around 9cm long. Make a small hook at the end of each length using your pliers.

2. Take a small piece of ivory flower paste and roll it into an elongated ball shape.

3. Dip the hooked end of the wire into edible glue and push it through the base of the ball shape into the centre of the bud. Twist the end so it is firmly attached to the wire and pinch off any excess.

4. Using the knife-modelling tool, make five indents from the top of the ball down the sides to form the centre bud. Leave to dry.

5. Make six buds for each flower stem. The buds should vary in size from 1-2cm. Leave these aside to dry.

FLOWERS

Central petal

6. The central petal (the labellum) of the flower is made up of four elements; the 'body', a 'head', two 'arms' and the diamond shape at the bottom, which we will cut to become two 'legs'.

7. Roll out some ivory flower paste, leaving a thick ridge in the centre. Place the labellum cutter with the top part centrally situated over the raised ridge and cut out, making sure you rub it firmly onto your workboard so there are no furry edges.

8. Flip this shape over and use your craft knife to make a central cut in the diamond shaped part to create the legs. Open the legs out slightly.

9. Place on the firm foam pad and use the small end of the ball tool to create an indent in the 'head'.

10. Use the larger end of the ball tool to soften and thin the edges, then for each 'arm' and 'leg' bring the ball tool to the centre, cupping and curving the petal.

11. Cut a length of no. 24 florist's wire into four, each 9cm long. Use the small pliers to bend 1cm into a right angle. Dip this into the edible glue, then push into the raised ridge on the back of the labellum.

12. Roll a tiny piece of flower paste into a flattish oval shape. Using the craft knife make a cut in the centre of the oval and gently pull it apart a tiny bit. Glue this shape onto the centre of the labellum.

The sepals and petals

13. Roll out some more ivory flower paste to about 1mm thick and cut out the three-part sepals.

14. Place this piece on top of the veiner and gently roll over with a small rolling pin to emboss the veins. Then place on the firm foam pad, and very lightly thin the edges with the ball tool.

15. Make a hole in the centre of one of the indents in the apple tray and put the sepals in this.

16. Cut, vein and thin two petals using the same process. Delicately glue the two petals so that they overlap slightly in centre of the sepals.

17. Paint a bit of edible glue on the back of the labellum and thread the wire through all layers.

ASSEMBLING A STEM

18. Take a short length of the florist's tape and stretch it to release the glue. Then, starting at the base of one bud, wrap the tape tightly around the wire.

19. As you will need quite a strong stem, take a length of no. 20 florist's wire and wrap the tape around both wires.

20. Take the next bud and attach to the stem about 1cm below the first bud by wrapping the tape around both wires. Continue in this way for another four buds, then add four orchid flowers.

Miniature Orchids

There is no need for cutters to make these simple mini orchids, and they can be used effectively on their own or as filler flowers to include in a bouquet.

Equipment needed

- / No. 26 florist's wire
- / Ivory flower paste
- / Edible glue (see p. 23)
- / Needle nose pliers
- / Firm foam pad
- / Ball tool
- / Pointed conical-ended modelling tool
- / Small paintbrush
- / Small scissors
- / Florist's tape

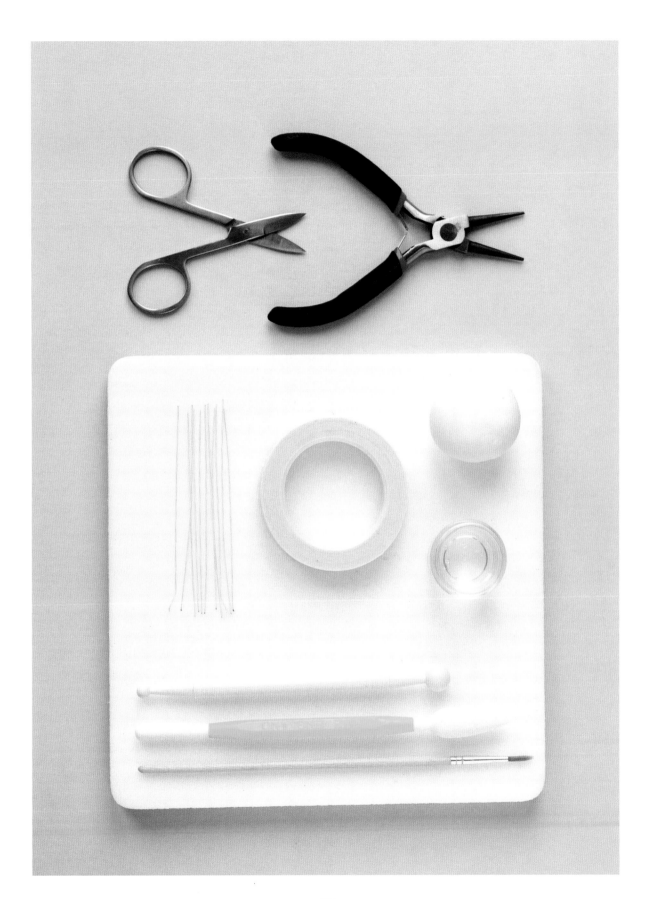

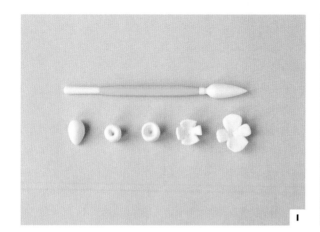

1

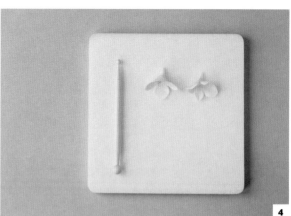

4

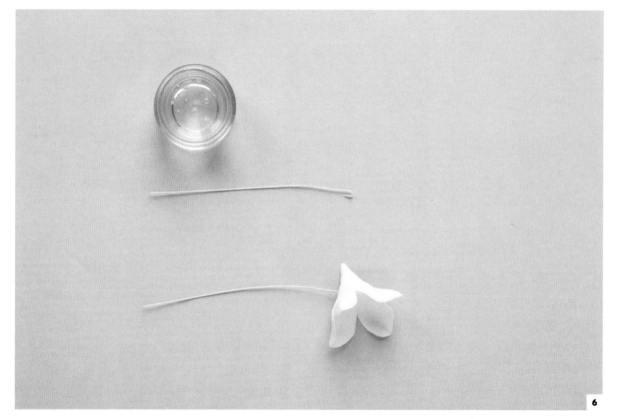

6

7b

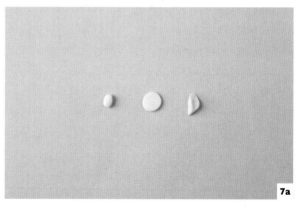

7a

1. Take a small ball of ivory flower paste and roll it into an elongated, conical shape.

2. Take the pointed conical-ended modelling tool and press into the wider end to indent it. Gently press and twist the modelling tool, opening up the indentation.

3. Make four incisions into this at the following clockface marks: 2.30 and 3.30 and 7.30 and 9.30. This will create two larger petals on the top and bottom, and smaller petals at the sides. Press each petal outwards gently with your fingers.

4. Place on the firm foam and use the ball tool to cup and thin each petal. Then pinch the tips of each petal into points.

5. Cut each wire into four lengths of 9cm each, and make a hook in the end of each with the pliers.

6. Dip the hooked end into edible glue and thread straight down through the centre of the blossom. Pinch off any excess from the pointed end of the flower.

7. For the centre, take a tiny ball of flower paste and squeeze it with your fingers to flatten it. Then pinch one end together and glue the pinched end in the centre of the orchid facing downwards.

8. To assemble a stem, take a short length of the florist's tape and stretch it to release the glue. Starting at the base of one flower, wrap the tape tightly around the wire. Then place the next flower 2cm down the wire and wrap the tape around them both. Continue in this way for four or five flowers.

SWEET
BRIAR ROSE

"I know a bank where the wild thyme blows,
Where oxslips and the nodding violet grows,
Quite over-canopied with luscious woodbine,
With sweet musk-roses, and with eglantine."
- A Midsummer Night's Dream,
William Shakespeare

This is a simple two-tier cake designed
with a fresh spring-like colour scheme of
ivory, primrose yellow and pale green. The
decoration is a wired garland of sweet briar
roses and leaves. Also known as eglantine,
the sweet briar rose is wild and rambling
with a sweet apple scent.

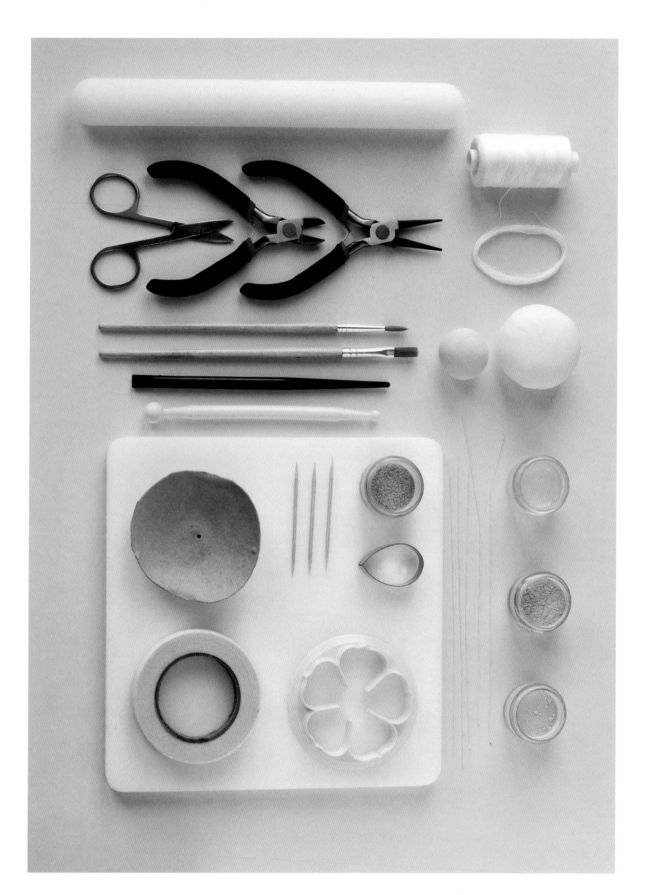

How To Make It

Techniques used

/ Making thread stamens

/ Making briar roses

/ Making rose leaves

/ Wiring a garland of roses and leaves

Equipment needed

/ White florist's tape

/ No. 22 florist's wire

FOR YOUR BASE STRUCTURE

Start with

- 1 x 20cm x 10cm cake
- 1 x 15cm x 7.5cm cake
- 1 x 25cm cake drum

1. Cover the tiers and the cake drum in ivory sugarpaste. Leave overnight to dry.

2. Attach the base (20cm) tier to the cake drum using royal icing, then dowel and stack the tiers.

3. Attach ribbon to the edge of the drum and on the base of each tier.

WIRED GARLAND

4. Make 11 sweet briar roses, 33 small rose leaves and nine medium rose leaves, following the instructions on p. 186.

5. Tape one rose to a length of no. 22 wire with florist's tape. Keep wrapping the tape around the wire for about 3cm, then attach another rose and a small cluster of leaves.

6. Keep attaching the roses and leaf clusters alternately, adding more lengths of no. 22 wire as needed. You're working towards a garland of roses and leaves measuring around 40cm long.

7. Carefully arrange this around the ledge of the cake, finishing on the top. You can secure the wire on the ledge by twisting the wire around itself, to hold it in place. If you're transporting the cake it might be wise to arrange this garland once the cake has been placed on the table.

Briar Rose and Leaves

Equipment needed

- / White florist's tape
- / No. 26 florist's wire
- / Small scissors
- / Cream flower paste
- / Pale green flower paste
- / White cotton thread
- / Edible glue (see p. 23)
- / Firm foam pad
- / Ball tool
- / Small non-stick rolling pin
- / Small paintbrush for glue
- / Small paintbrush for dusting
- / Pink petal dust
- / 65mm five-petal rose cutter
- / Dry semolina
- / Veining tool
- / Small non-stick rolling pin
- / Small and medium sized rose leaf cutters
- / Rose leaf veiner

1

6

9

12

11

13

STAMENS

1. Cut a piece of no. 26 florist's wire into two equal lengths. Fold one length of wire in half and twist very near the top to create a small loop.

2. Wrap the cotton thread 25 times around three fingers of one hand. Take the thread off your fingers and twist in the centre.

3. Thread the wire through the twisted centre, bring it up to the loop and then twist the wire again, securing the thread.

4. Trim the thread to 2cm, then secure with florist's tape, wrapping it to start halfway over the loop of wire. You should now have a broom-like shape.

5. Separate the cotton threads with a pin, paint edible glue on the very ends and then dip in semolina, so that you end up with clumps of little balls at the ends of the threads.

6. Dust the cotton and ends with a primrose-coloured dust and separate the threads again.

7. Paint edible glue on the small loop of wire at the top and glue a small ball of pale green flower paste onto this for the centre. Give it texture by making small pricks with a cocktail stick.

PETALS

8. Roll out the cream flower paste thinly and cut out a rose shape with the 65mm five-petal rose cutter.

9. Use the petal cutter to trim a little indent from the top centre of each petal, so that they are almost heart-shaped.

10. Place the petals on the firm foam pad and use the ball tool to thin out the edges. Then roll the veining tool over each petal to create texture.

ATTACHING THE CENTRES

11. Paint edible glue onto the centre of the petals and thread the wired centre and stamens through.

12. Pinch the underside of the flower to secure it to the wire. Then take a small ball of cream flower paste and thread it onto the wire, securing it to the underside of the flower, so that it forms a calyx.

13. Make a hole in the centre of an indent in an apple tray. Place the wire through this so the rose is resting in the indented section. Leave to dry.

ROSE LEAVES

14. Flatten a small piece of pale green paste with your fingers.

15. Roll out both sides from the centre leaving a thicker ridge in the centre of the paste. Place the rose leaf cutter with the centre over the ridge, and cut.

16. Cut the no. 28 florist's wire into four equal lengths. Dip the end of one length into the edible glue and carefully push it about 1cm up the thick centre ridge. Pinch the paste at the very base of the leaf to make sure it's secured firmly to the wire.

17. Press firmly onto the rose leaf veiner. Then thin the edges of the leaf using the ball tool on the firm foam pad. Leave to dry.

MAKING LEAF CLUSTERS

18. Stretch the florist's tape to release the glue and tape the wires of the leaves together in eight clusters of three small leaves and three clusters of five medium leaves.

Jazz Age templates

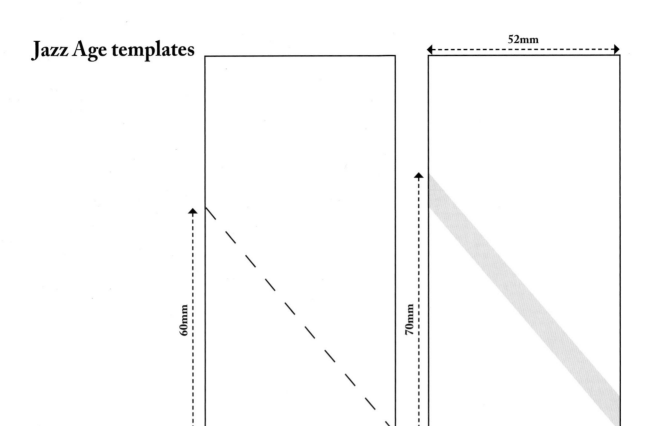

52mm

60mm

70mm

Enchanted Forest templates

Art Deco templates

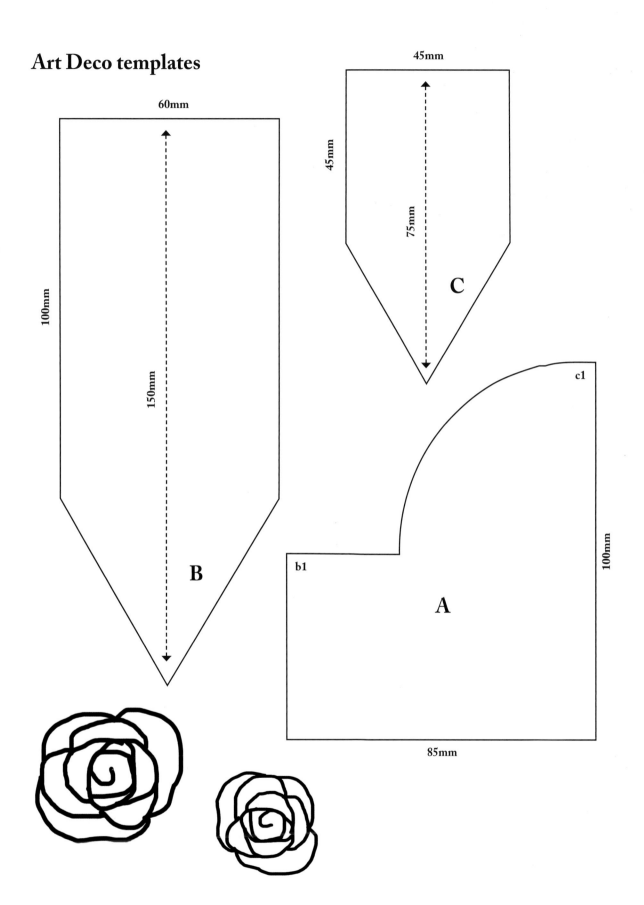

60mm

100mm

150mm

B

45mm

45mm

75mm

C

c1

b1

100mm

A

85mm

Acknowledgements

Many thanks to everyone who has helped in some way or another with my cake journey and this book, but especially to my daughter Yasmine, and sister Julie.

Thanks also to my fantastic publisher, Ziggy and Diana and Garry for the wonderful photography.

Published by Cicada Books Limited
Text by Rosalind Miller
Photography by Garry Maclennan and Diana Chaccour
Styling by Clare Nicolson
Design by April

British Library Cataloguing-in-Publication Data.

A CIP record for this book is available from the British Library.
ISBN: 978-1-908714-08-4

Cicada Books Limited
48 Burghley Road
London NW5 1UE
T: +44 207 209 2259
ziggy@cicadabooks.co.uk
www.cicadabooks.co.uk